"John Ebrahimian's introduction to mimetic theory is outstanding for its warm, lively, conversational tone and for its memorable, illustrative examples. Reading it, one is easily drawn into an atmosphere that recalls Ebrahimian's own life-changing talks with René Girard on topics that affect us all: love, desire, envy, violence, redemption. Highly recommended."

—ANN W. ASTELL, John Cardinal O'Hara Professor of Theology, University of Notre Dame

"As the extraordinary work of theorist René Girard becomes more widely known, the need for a clear, user-friendly, introductory account of each of his major ideas—with extended materials for further critical study—becomes increasingly pressing. With chapters on mimetic desire, on collective violence and the scapegoat mechanism, and on the role of Jewish and Christian scriptural texts in addressing these topics in ancient and modern cultural settings, this exciting book fills that need superbly."

—SANDOR GOODHART, Professor Emeritus of English and Jewish Studies, Purdue University

"Ebrahimian's introduction to the thought of René Girard is clear, useful, and honest, presented in an engaged personal voice but without any posturing. It never wavers from Girard's simple directive which I heard him give to a conference at Innsbruck University who asked him what we can do to keep mimetic theory ongoing and influential: 'We search for the truth; nothing else matters.'"

—WILLIAM A. JOHNSEN, editor, *Contagion: The Journal of The Colloquium on Violence and Religion*

"This guide to René Girard for 'newbies' sets a conversational tone from its first pages. Whether you settle in with this book over a morning cup of Joe or select it from your nightstand, your curiosity about big topics in human life—love, war, envy, and violence—will be rewarded. *How Violence Works* explains how desire in human life leads to conflict and violence but also is capable of producing good. Offering examples from daily life, popular culture, and well-known works of literature, the book invites you to think more deeply about your own life in order to replace envy and rivalry with compassionate relationships. A timely and welcome contribution to books about mimetic theory."

—MARTHA J. REINEKE, Professor of Religion Emeritus,
University of Northern Iowa

How Violence Works

How Violence Works

An Introduction to René Girard's Mimetic Theory

JOHN BABAK EBRAHIMIAN

CASCADE *Books* • Eugene, Oregon

HOW VIOLENCE WORKS
An Introduction to René Girard's Mimetic Theory

Copyright © 2025 John Babak Ebrahimian. All rights reserved. Except for brief quotations in critical publications or reviews, no part of this book may be reproduced in any manner without prior written permission from the publisher. Write: Permissions, Wipf and Stock Publishers, 199 W. 8th Ave., Suite 3, Eugene, OR 97401.

Cascade Books
An Imprint of Wipf and Stock Publishers
199 W. 8th Ave., Suite 3
Eugene, OR 97401

www.wipfandstock.com

PAPERBACK ISBN: 979-8-3852-3457-8
HARDCOVER ISBN: 979-8-3852-3458-5
EBOOK ISBN: 979-8-3852-3459-2

Cataloguing-in-Publication data:

Names: Ebrahimian, John Babak, author.

Title: How violence works : an introduction to René Girard's mimetic theory / John Babak Ebrahimian.

Description: Eugene, OR : Cascade Books, 2025 | Includes bibliographical references.

Identifiers: ISBN 979-8-3852-3457-8 (paperback) | ISBN 979-8-3852-3458-5 (hardcover) | ISBN 979-8-3852-3459-2 (ebook)

Subjects: LCSH: Girard, René, 1923–2015. | Memetics. | Theology.

Classification: B2430.G494 .E27 2025 (paperback) | B2430.G494 .E27 (ebook)

05/12/25

All black and white and color images are from the Metropolitan Museum of Art's Open Access Initiative and in the Public Domain.

Contents

Preface		ix
Acknowledgments		xiii
1	What Is Desire?	1
2	Doubles and the Mimetic Crisis	19
3	Metaphysical Desire, Contagion, and the Mimetic Crisis	39
4	The Sacrificial Crisis and the Scapegoat Mechanism	52
5	"And the Solution Is: Sacrifice 'em": Myth	69
6	From Scapegoats to Deliverance: Episodes from Genesis and the Hebrew Bible	84
7	The Sacrifice to End all Sacrifices: The Account of Jesus's Passion in the Gospels	108
Conclusion: The End of Violence		127
A Brief Glossary of Mimetic Theory		141
A Biographical Introduction to René Girard		147
Bibliography		151

For René

Preface

EVERY SO OFTEN AN individual comes along whose thought and existence provides the basis of a 180-degree revolution in a person, a field, a country, or an era. The result is a complete transformation in a person or a landscape of thought into a new one. This book comes out of my encounter with the interdisciplinary thinker René Girard, an internationally known academic and public intellectual who in 2005 was awarded the highest honor of being an "Immortal" in the Académie française in his native country of France.

Girard has made profound contributions to the study of literature, anthropology, religion, and psychology. Over the last six decades he has revolutionized these fields of study with his challenging ideas. But his influence has not just remained within higher education. His thought has been picked up, applied, and extended by practitioners in many fields and helping professions as well. As a Catholic thinker (but by no means limited as one), he has influenced theology and practice in the Christian church and in other faith traditions. Yet he has engaged with the highest level of intellectuals, professionals of many types, and political figures, especially in North America, France, and Europe. In France, his books were even on the bestseller lists. The French president, Emmanuel Jean-Michel Frédéric Macron is known to have quoted Girard from his last book, *Battling to the End*. But what is René Girard about? That's what this book seeks to explain.

Since meeting and working with him many years ago, one of my passions has been to introduce non-specialists to Girard's work. This means making it accessible while still doing justice to the complexity of his thought. To make it easy, I will start with how I personally met him. It was the summer of 1992 while I was a graduate student at Stanford University, and I had finished my requirements for theater directing in the department of drama. Being an enthusiast of literary theory, I had taken most of the literary theory classes the school had to offer except those taught by Professor Girard, who at that time was the Andrew B. Hammond Professor of French Literature, Language and Culture (with a joint appointment in the two departments of comparative literature and religion) at Stanford. He was already well-known on campus and indeed around the world at that time.

I had seen Girard on a French television episode, called *Apostrophe* while I lived in France, but never dared to contact him to see what his theory was all about. This changed that summer when I summoned up my courage, walked into his secretary's office, and asked to make an appointment, which I was given one afternoon later that week. That request and meeting changed my life. And rather than one meeting, it became a series of meetings that whole summer long.

By this time I had read parts of Girard's major books which laid out a theory of literature, anthropology, religion, and psychology, with applications in many other fields as well. In those first meetings I wanted to discuss what I thought I knew something about: the theater, Antonin Artaud, Artaud's theater of cruelty, mythology according to Artaud, and various plays by William Shakespeare. Professor Girard was relaxed and often had a smile or laugh on his face while he answered my questions. As I asked questions, listened attentively and got to know him, my courage grew to ask him about his own thought and books: I had *Violence and the Sacred* in one hand and *Things Hidden Since the Foundation of the World* in another. Discussing his work, we soon shifted to sitting outside in the cafeteria area where we could talk about his books in a more relaxed atmosphere over coffee or lunch.

Professor Girard was a gift: he knew about almost everything and did not hesitate to share and discuss any subject with his students or anyone else who wanted to engage in dialogue. Our summer discussions went beyond my expectations or belief. I asked him about desire; I asked him about love; I challenged him about war and peace, referring to literature or the day's news; and eventually I asked about God. Knowing well that he was one of a minority of intellectuals at Stanford who believed in God, at one point, I directly challenged him and asked: "Professor Girard, if you say God exists, then why did God let World War II happen?" He seriously answered my question, giving his unique perspective.

Whatever topic I touched on, whether about life or literature and culture, he answered with a warm smile or a wholehearted laughter. He

Preface

was a delight to be around. I had met some giant thinkers and geniuses before, but none had ever touched and influenced me as much as Girard had, that summer and for the rest of my life. By the end of the summer, we had become very well acquainted, and during the following terms at Stanford when he taught courses on his thought, I had the honor of serving as his teaching assistant. And I have continued to study and teach him to this day.

The hallmark of a genius is that his thought keeps evolving. This was and is the case with René Girard; he never stopped thinking or writing, and each book opened a new door and shed light onto a new horizon of inquiry, providing a new chapter of his thoughts on life and humanity. Though he died in 2015, like Einstein he has become immortal. This book has been a joy and challenge to write. It has been written for an audience that is intelligent and curious about almost everything. This would include graduate students, professionals of all types, parents, high school and college students, and anyone with great curiosity about life but who is not necessarily an academic specialist. Girard's universe was and is as interesting and complex as Einstein's was, and like Einstein's universe where his thought could be reduced to its essence of the formula $E=mc^2$, Girard's starts and ends with the simple concept of "mimetic desire." We will unpack this concept from its beginning to its logical end, as he did in his long career. As he claimed about his thought: "Mimetic desire is a simple concept capable of explaining many complex things," and "It's just a hypothesis, prove it wrong if you can." He was always open to new insight and loved a good challenge.

René Girard was a very modest and humble man, but also a towering figure. As many have claimed, he was larger than life. A great deal has already been written about Girard, his life, and his thought, and I am very grateful for that. This book aims to introduce him to yet another audience. It will take the reader through the basics of Girard's thought and mimetic theory step by step, with many examples from popular culture, politics, literature, Shakespeare, mythology, and religion. I have included reflection questions at the end of each chapter to help the reader process and discuss the material. In addition, key terms and concepts are bolded the first time they appear in the text and can be found in the Glossary. My hope is that my book will not only introduce the reader to the mimetic theory and the thoughts of René Girard but also start them on a life-long quest for insight and knowledge, in the same way he influenced me.

Acknowledgments

I WOULD FIRST AND foremost like to thank Professor René Girard, whose visionary thinking is responsible for mimetic theory. I am most thankful for his guidance throughout the early stages of the book. My extreme gratitude also extends to Martha Girard, his wife, whose encouragement was an invaluable source of support.

I am grateful to my Girardian colleagues and editors, Rebecca Adams and Br. Anthony Zuba, Capuchin, whose meticulous reading and insightful editing helped shape the final version of this book. My gratitude also extends to Charlie Collier and his editorial team at Wipf and Stock Publishers for their generous support and steady guidance.

I am also indebted to the international scholars and members of the Colloquium on Violence and Religion (COV&R), who gather annually to discuss new developments and discoveries in mimetic theory. In presenting my ideas at these meetings, I have been fortunate to receive invaluable feedback and intellectual camaraderie. In particular, I would like to thank Jean-Pierre Dupuy, Joel Hodge, Sandor Goodhart, and Martha Reineke for their engaged responses and ongoing dialogue.

The first round of the feedback on the manuscript was generously provided by Leila Dehghani-Valazzi, Alaleh Ebrahimian, Kurt A. Jordan, David Porter, Alex Young and Susan Wagner. I am sincerely grateful for the care and rigor they brought to their readings.

I would also like to express my immense gratitude to Shadi Bartch-Zimmer, Fr. Francis Belanger, OP, Akbar and Roshanak Etemad, Mary Keating, Chuck Lin, Fr. Ugo Nacciaroene, SJ, Michael G. Nichols, Laura Rodriguez, David Valazzi, Luigi Valazzi, and Marica Valazzi, all of whom played a very supportive role at various stages of the process.

Acknowledgments

Last but not least, I would like to extend my gratitude to my parents, Mehdi and Violette Ebrahimian, whose encouragement to write this book came from a desire to better understand mimetic theory for themselves.

1

What Is Desire?

LOVE. WAR. ENVY. VIOLENCE. Where do these come from?

There's a force at work in human nature. It's behind us, before us, around us. From youth to old age, it animates our thoughts and directs our actions. It shapes every person, every people, every society, every culture. It's been with us from the beginning of human civilization. It could also be the end of human civilization. But we couldn't be human without it. It's the source of our creativity and compassion. It's also the source of our hatred, and it stokes our insatiable appetite for destruction. Without it, we will never achieve happiness. If we don't learn how to use it wisely, we are sure to perish.

What is this force? For an answer, let's look to the fundamental insights of the interdisciplinary thinker René Girard, whose work we will be unpacking in this book. Girard was one of the most important thinkers of the twentieth century, and his thought begins and ends with the fundamental concept of desire.

DESIRE

Let's talk about desire.

Girard believes desire is the quintessential human phenomenon. It sets us apart from every other animal. Indeed, it's the force that gives rise to human nature and governs our behaviors.

All creatures have needs. By instinct animals identify their needs and fulfill them. They do this by copying the behavior of other members of the herd. Generally, members of a herd fulfill their needs without undermining the survival of the whole. By instinct they resolve competition over limited goods—food, mating partners—in non-conflictive ways. Instinct holds them in check. Humans are different. Somewhere in the course of our evolution, the mechanism for identifying and satisfying our needs surpassed the limits of instinct and crossed over a threshold to a realm of greater complexity and magnitude. Our capacity to identify with those whose behaviors we copied to meet our needs lost all restraint. The mere satisfaction of needs was overtaken by an unquenchable longing for more. In other words, needs mutated into wants. An irrepressible, insatiable urge took possession of this species. It was the birth of desire. It was the birth of the human.

We're interested here in the way this human desire works. We're interested in what sets human desire apart from mere satisfaction of instinctual drives, turns hunger into cravings, and turns needs into wants. René Girard's **mimetic theory** explores these questions.

IMITATION

Let's talk about imitation.

When we talk about human desire, we're always talking about imitative desire. Girard uses a special phrase: **mimetic desire**. The word *mimetic* is derived from *mimesis*, the Greek word for imitation. Mimetic desire means wanting through imitation. Simply put, we want what the other person wants.

Think about yourself for a moment. Think about your favorite things: certain foods, certain clothes, or certain songs or movies or places. Did you ever wonder how you came to like those things so much? Didn't someone you know introduce them to you? Didn't their own preferences move you to adopt those things as your very own? What makes those things so very special to you? We can find many great works of art and many fine foods in the world. What makes your preferences valuable to you? Could it be that it isn't only the merits of the things in themselves, but also your relationship to the other persons who brought them to your attention?

Or consider this. Can you ever remember a time when you were carefree and content? Or rather, have you always carried one preoccupation after another like an invisible sack? What's on your mind? Let's put aside for a moment worries like sickness or poverty. These are global problems. Let's turn from the world for a moment and look at ourselves in our intimate, anxious thoughts. Consider these: the hostility you feel toward the new student in your Spanish class who speaks more fluently than you do; the resentment you feel as the understudy toward the lead actor in the musical you're rehearsing; the pressure you feel to get your GPA above your classmates who are vying for the same college fund scholarship. Or consider the admiration and jealousy you feel toward your good friend who could afford that new smartphone, even though you have a smartphone capable of doing everything you need. Or consider any time in your childhood when your parents favored your siblings over you with more dessert, more play time, better birthday presents. You may think your preoccupations occur without rhyme or reason, but this isn't true. You may not be aware of it, but there's nothing accidental about your thoughts, feelings, and emotions. It's the mechanism of mimetic desire that triggers them.

Now, let's make a map of desire. Let's draw a triangle.

TRIANGULAR DESIRE

Girard tells us that human desire is never linear. It doesn't just proceed from the needy person directly to the thing needed. Instead, one person identifies what she needs through another person who has attained or is seeking that certain something. Thus desire is angular.

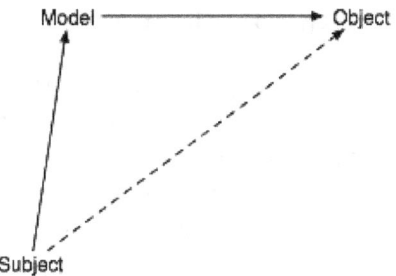

Fig. 1 Triangular Desire

It bends mere needs into wants. Another person (what Girard calls the **model** or the **mediator**) stands between the one who desires and the thing or object that person wants. In fact, I want the object because the other wants it!

We can visualize desire as "triangular," with the desiring person or **subject** forming one point of the triangle, the model of imitation (the person they imitate) forming the second point, and the **object** of desire (hinted at or desired by the model) forming the third and endpoint.

It's as simple as that! A model whom we respect, admire and love secretly or openly suggests objects of desire which we want for ourselves. We may regard this person so highly that we may even copy their behaviors and mannerisms consciously.

This is not to say that every choice we make is conditioned by others. If you're hungry and all you can find is a jar of peanut butter, then you will have peanut butter. If you're crossing a barren desert and you're thirsty, then you will make a beeline to the first jug of water you see. We're not talking about instinctual bodily appetites. We're talking about something more complex than basic stimulus-response. We're talking about a socially conditioned response to goods that we don't necessarily need. Girard believes it's not the goods themselves but the individuals we look to who make them attractive to us, who are the stimulus. They exert a force as strong as gravity over us. Therefore, our responses aren't merely instinctual. Our responses are mimetic, imitative, by nature, and dynamic. Our seeing passes through another person's eyes. What the second person, the "model," chooses becomes our choice. So our choices aren't just subject-object. They are subject-model-object. That's desire!

THE POWER OF MODELS

In mimetic desire we have a simple principle by which we can understand the behaviors of consumers as well as the dynamics of whole societies and nations. Consumerism is the principle of mimetic desire made into an economic doctrine. Because of mimetic desire, even primary needs can be converted into wants. The existence of countless varieties of bottled water sold under dozens of brand names can't be accounted for by thirst alone. Potable water is a need; but bottled water is a want. It's a product of desire. When faced with an abundance of products, we have no way of resolving how to choose among them without resorting to imitation of other people. We fall back on the influence of other people who teach us how to choose. However we choose the bottled water—for its affordability (or, to the contrary, its costliness because we seek luxury), its flavor, its carbonation (or lack of carbonation), its lack of calories—we choose because of the values other people model for us. When we choose a certain product, we aren't really choosing the product. We're choosing the model who already chose for us. The model mediates our choices.

You don't believe it?

Then why do celebrities get paid handsomely to promote beverages? If a product could sell itself, then why waste advertising dollars on human sponsors? There's a reason why supermodels sell lingerie, and it has nothing to do with demonstrating the comfort or utility of the underwear. The jug of water in the desert may say "water" to the thirst-stricken wanderer. But that same water, carefully bottled and advertised, then sold in the social-economic spaces we call supermarkets, will gain a different value and meaning according to who sponsors it and how many people we know are drinking it. Bottled water doesn't just say "water." It says "Maria Sharapova," or some other celebrity name, whom we can recognize and look to. Girard makes clear that the object may not even be that important; rather, we want to imitate the model, have what the model has, even become, sometimes, what the model *is*. Desire is about fascination with the model.

It should be clear by now why we call the second person in our triangle of desire the model. The model is someone we admire and look up to, someone who effortlessly communicates values to us. Even without taking any conscious steps toward control of the subject, the model does in fact exert control by mediating the needs of the subject. The second person conditions the choices of the first person. The subject-model-object interaction is the basic dynamic of mimetic desire.[1] It gives birth to desire, provides its definition, sustains its force, and predicts its shifts and movements. The model is critical as the source of desire.

All of this derives from René Girard's key insight into human nature. It's fashionable nowadays to believe that each of us is an autonomous

---

1. Girard discovered mimetic desire through the reading and analysis of five European writers—Dostoyevsky, Proust, Flaubert, Cervantes, and Stendhal whose books served as the foundation and center of his first book, *Deceit, Desire and the Novel*. His concept of psychology, called "interdividual psychology," gained formal formulation in his book *Things Hidden Since the Foundation of the World*, where in a dialogue and collaboration with psychiatrist Jean-Michael Oughourlian the idea of understanding the self through others was developed. See Book III of *Things Hidden Since the Foundation of the World*.

individual. Each of us alone is in control of our choices. But desire often doesn't come from ourselves. It's so often derived from someone else.

AN INFINITY OF MEDIATION

The triangle of desire is at work everywhere you find people and social situations. The triangle of desire fits so many social patterns you can find because the triangle is about people influencing people. Everyone can be a subject. Everyone can be a model. At home, the infant (subject) mimics the sounds and gestures (object) of her parents (model). The child (subject), looking up at his parent (model) reading the newspaper (object), grabs the newspaper. A person whose favorite grandparent was kind or mean may learn to be kind or mean. As children develop, they find new models other than their parents. The adolescents (subject) look to their classmates (model) to decide what kind of clothes they want to wear (object), what car to drive (object), which college to attend (object).

Every choice we make, big or small, is typically mediated by another person. The possibilities are endless:

- a daughter (subject) learns from her mother (model) how to stand up for her rights (object);
- a son (s) follows his father (m) into a career in medicine (o);
- a student (s) mimics their French teacher (m) and adopts a French accent (o);
- one twin girl (s) practices like Simone Biles (m) in a quest to be a great gymnast (o)
- her twin sister (s) practices like Caitlin Clark (m) to become a great basketball player (o);
- a young person (s) reads *The Autobiography of Malcolm X* (m) and joins the Nation of Islam (o) or reads Dr. Martin Luther King Jr. and joins a civil rights campaign; another reads *Mein Kampf* (m) and joins a neo-Nazi group (o);
- a young woman (s) imitates Taylor Swift (m) in fashion, mannerism, and style (o).

What Is Desire?

As the examples above demonstrate, the mediation can be either positive or negative. In fact, it's easy to find examples of mediation all around us. Let's look at some more of them.

DESIRE, LITERATURE AND POPULAR CULTURE

One of the best ways to learn how desire works among people and in society is to look at great works of literature. Literature, like the other arts, is a mirror of everyday life. Girard argues that what we find in the great characters of literature—heroes, villains, madmen, lovers—can be a distilled or more polished version of our own lives. We can look to great literature as well as examples in popular culture to learn about ourselves. Let's look at one episode in Mark Twain's *Tom Sawyer* and several others in situations familiar to us all to shed light on the imitative nature of desire and how it functions at a primary level.

You may remember Mark Twain's famous tale. Because he has gotten into a fight, Aunt Polly grounds Tom Sawyer. His punishment is to spend his Saturday whitewashing the fence. Tom's *not* looking forward to this labor. As the boys walk by the fence, Tom feels less and less motivated to do the work. Then comes a bright idea: "At this dark and hopeless moment an inspiration burst upon him! Nothing less than a great, magnificent inspiration."[2] Tom begins to pretend he's having a good time. Ben, one of the neighborhood boys who Tom dreads, arrives at the scene, imitating the steamboat *Big Missouri*. Tom continues his whitewashing in a casual and deliberate manner. He doesn't respond to Ben's pokes, insults, and queries. He pretends to be uninterested in Ben and totally absorbed in painting the fence. He transforms his chore into play. Ben watches Tom whitewashing and wants to join in. Tom doesn't allow him. This makes Ben want all the more to paint the fence. The more Ben asks, the more Tom raises the prohibition and the stakes, making the work even more desirable to Ben. He begs Tom: "Say, Tom, let *me* whitewash a little."[3] Tom responds: "Does a boy get a chance to whitewash a fence every day?" Tom (the model) concocts a story to make the whitewashing (the object) appear to be a special task difficult to attain or achieve, a sacred duty he doesn't have the power to give up. He teases his subject: "Ben, I'd like to . . . but Aunt Polly—well, Jim wanted to do it, but she wouldn't let him; Sid wanted to do it, and she wouldn't let

---

2. Twain, *Tom Sawyer*, 23.
3. Twain, *Tom Sawyer*, 24.

Sid. Now don't you see how I'm fixed? If you was to tackle this fence and anything was to happen to it—."[4]

Ben bargains with Tom, offering him the core of his apple in exchange for the fence. Tom, knowing full well Ben is caught in his trap, plays hard to get. He holds out. His refusal pays off: Ben offers Tom the entire apple. Finally, Tom "reluctantly" gives up the brush. And Ben gives up being a steamship for whitewashing the fence. He's only the first victim. "Tom gave up the brush with reluctance in his face, but alacrity in his heart. And while the late steamer Big Missouri worked and sweated in the sun, the retired artist sat on a barrel in the shade close by, dangled his legs, munched his apple, and planned the slaughter of more innocents. There was no lack of material; boys happened along every little while; they came to jeer, but remained to whitewash."[5] Tom Sawyer's trick worked on every boy: "He had had a nice, good, idle time all the while—plenty of company—and the fence had three coats of whitewash on it! If he hadn't run out of whitewash he would have bankrupted every boy in the village." Twain concludes this fable of desire with a moral: "Tom said to himself that it was not such a hollow world, after all. He had discovered a great law of human action, without knowing it—namely, that in order to make a man or a boy covet a thing, it is only necessary to make the thing difficult to attain."[6]

A model can make an object desirable in many ways. The model can present the object as something precious or rare. In *Tom Sawyer* Twain observes that we desire those things that are hard to get. In reality these objects may not be precious, rare, or difficult to obtain after all. But in the dynamic of triangular desire, the model stands between the subject and the object of desire. The perception that the model communicates, either consciously or unconsciously, to the subject that such an object is precious, rare, and hard to get becomes reality for that person.

DESIRE AND EXTERNAL MEDIATION

Girard explores in detail how imitation works among individuals and within culture. He makes a distinction between what he calls **external mediation** and **internal mediation.** In both cases, the subject imitates the model, but different results happen. In internal mediation, Girard shows how the

---

4. Twain, *Tom Sawyer*, 25.
5. Twain, *Tom Sawyer*, 25.
6. Twain, *Tom Sawyer*, 26.

What Is Desire?

subject can become consumed by desire. Sometimes this tension is so great it leads to conflict and violence between the model, the source of desire, and the subject who imitates the model, because they want the same object. Girard uses the image of two hands reaching for the same thing. How can admiration between the subject and the model turn into hatred and rivalry? We'll talk about this dynamic of internal mediation, very important to Girard's thinking, shortly. But for now, let's look at external mediation, where the subject can imitate the model without dominating or undermining the model.

In external mediation, there's no conflict between the subject and the model and there's no direct rivalry over an object that cannot be shared. This dynamic remains peaceful because the subject and the model are a safe distance from one another—their social spheres are too far apart for them to really compete over the same exact objects. There's no threat from one to the other. Each person pursues their mutually desired object without interference from the other. In fact, "The hero of external mediation proclaims aloud the true nature of his [imitated] desire. He worships his models openly and declares himself his disciple."[7] There will be no danger at hand, so long as the subject copies the model from a distance, thereby never imposing a direct threat to the model by trying to take away the same object. That's because in these cases the model's objects of desire are just too far away to be attained: the subject and model don't live in the same social world or on the same plane. Yet the subject can imitate the model's general desires and characteristics, and this may lead to positive results.

It's easy to find examples of external mediation all around us. Let's look at a few more. Apart from examples of great literature—which reveal mimetic desire in a manner that often mirrors real life—external mediation exists in countless everyday situations, including popular culture such as film, television, sports teams, athletic figures, and the worlds of fashion, advertising and marketing. Remaining at a distance from their subjects, the realms of both sports and film can easily create and foster "stars" and "heroes" for their subject/admirers. Popular actors, actresses and athletic figures can easily be transformed into super-models and super-heroes by the mechanism of external mediation. We can see the formation of positive mimesis created by the external model in the description of six-time National Basketball Association (NBA) championship winner, Michael Jordan, by one of his admirers:

7. Girard, *Deceit, Desire and the Novel*, 10.

> Michael Jordan is my hero for many reasons. He was a great basketball player. In his busy schedule, he always found time to give back. He was not greedy with his money. He always worked hard at everything that he did. He was very determined and never gave up. He always found a way to triumph in any situation. He always found time to spend with his family. All of these things make him one of the greatest heroes of all time.[8]

Perhaps as influential as sports, the film industry also has the capability to create stars and heroes worldwide through external mediation. Movies, by definition, are an externally mediated enterprise inviting audiences to live within the realm of the film being watched. Actors and actresses and the roles they portray provide models of imitation. Figures like Humphrey Bogart, James Dean, Marlon Brando, Audrey Hepburn, and Marilyn Monroe have all become cultural icons and cult figures. Today, we still imitate or admire their ways of speaking, walking, talking and even smoking. New stars arise all the time for our admiration and emulation. Every teenager has had pictures of the latest band, group or solo artist on their bedroom walls.

For the most part, don't be afraid of external mediation. It's often a good thing, as it's a powerful motivational force. Its benefits to society are incalculable. It's the engine of human productivity. Think of how many distinguished artists, engineers, physicians, and political leaders were born out of admiration of great figures who proceeded them. Constructive forms of mimetic desire fuel ambition, or aspiration, and when properly mediated and channeled, can bring about many affirmative results. External mediation can generate an ever-expanding array of positive role models whose contributions to justice, peace, and the common good create a virtuous cycle of admiration and imitation, plus the proliferation of material and metaphysical (or less tangible) goods. In external mediation we have heroes, and we aspire to their achievements, to be like them.

External mediation may not always lead to a more productive life and positive achievements, though. It could also lead to futility. The teenager who idolizes their model—a celebrated movie star, rock singer, or political leader—is being mediated by that ideal image of the model who's far away. In external mediation the distance between the model and the subject remains so great, and the object desired (an Academy Award, or a number one song, the Presidency) remains so lofty and remote, it's unlikely to be attained. There's little the subject can do, as the model can only be worshipped

---

8. Nuest, "Michael Jordan," para. 9.

and idolized from afar. So there's little to be gained from the imitation. On the other hand, there's little risk of conflict between the two. The subject can't ever take the model's place, and the model can't ever be threatened by the subject. External mediation may consign the subject to a fruitless life of chasing after dreams. Girard talks at length about the amusing example of external mediation found in the famous novel by Cervantes, *Don Quixote*. You're probably already familiar with the story. Don Quixote reads novels of lofty chivalric romance and takes as his ideal model a fictional knight named Amadis of Gaul. Quixote wants to fight other knights in battles and rescue damsels just like his idol, and he tries to do so in his everyday environment, which leads to humorous and absurd results.

Don Quixote and Sancho Panza
Honoré Daumier—French, nineteenth century

But Quixote can never truly compete with his hero Amadis of Gaul, and the things Amadis desires prove too far away or so vague as to be unattainable. Like children and their parents, Quixote and Amadis don't occupy the same social sphere or plane of existence. But Quixote tries anyway. In the end, Quixote repents on his deathbed of his absurd dreams derived from reading chivalric novels. They haven't led to any apparent serious harm, yet they have caused him to waste his life and perhaps inspired others to do equally absurd things which waste time.

We have another example of external mediation at a distance in the volunteer who campaigns for a candidate, putting up posters, knocking on doors, calling voters. By and by, the volunteer may begin to dream of higher office for themselves, which may or may not be realistic. The candidate mediates the subject, with the candidate as the ideal and exemplar, the person she wants to be one day. At this moment there may be a lot of distance between themselves and the candidate. Right now the subject can't ever take the place of that leader: the gap between them remains so vast that there is no possibility of competition. In such a situation, the subject will always love and idolize her hero, but the hero will remain forever untouchable. The subject can't attain the objects such a mediator desires, so no rivalry ensues. Or the person may attain an object similar to, but not directly conflicting with, that of the model. More than one person can hold political office of some kind, for instance.

External mediation is often harmless. Given the right circumstances with the right models, it's capable of creating healthy desires and good results. Because you never know. Some will recall a famous photograph of Bill Clinton as a teenager shaking hands with President John F. Kennedy. What does the young Clinton think of at this moment? Is he thinking about this president, or the presidency itself? Is he thinking not only that he could be *like this president*, but also that he could *be the president*? When we look at this photo, we know both men only as distant historical figures, but may find ourselves having similar thoughts or aspirations. Out of such dreams, sometimes real achievements are born.

While external mediation of heroes and stars can provide positive or neutral role models, in some situations it can be destructive through negative examples. For instance, in 1972 filmmaker Stanley Kubrick outlawed the screening in London of his dystopian, graphic and controversial film *A Clockwork Orange* after a sixty-one-week run, because violent youth-gangs began identifying with the film's characters, creating a violent **contagion** of rapes and gang wars:

> In the year after the movie's cinematic release in 1971, a number of disturbing crimes were reported that seemed to have connections with some of its most infamous and disturbing scenes. It appeared as if some copy-cats were on the loose.

In perhaps the most shocking of these incidents, a group of men from Lancashire assaulted a 17-year-old girl to the tune of "Singin' in the Rain,"

What Is Desire?

mirroring the brutal scene near the beginning of the movie in the abandoned building.

> In addition, according to The Telegraph, a 16-year-old boy was found guilty of killing an elderly homeless man, after claiming that he had heard about a similar scene in the movie. The association of real-world acts of violence with the movie was deeply upsetting for Kubrick, and he decided to pull *A Clockwork Orange* from the British market.[9]

As the Telegraph reported, "[T]he hysteria created around the release of A Clockwork Orange had potentially rendered the film dangerous. Several of the perpetrators of the crimes that were supposedly imitating the film had not even seen it—they had simply heard descriptions of the acts. The scandal itself was becoming more dangerous than the content of the movie." The power of external mimetic desire shouldn't be underestimated. Subjects are easily suggestable. We can find both good and bad models to imitate. What the subject sees, hears and thus desires from the model can easily produce peace and virtues—or negativity and destruction—through a process of contagion.

Similar to the external mediation that operates throughout the fashion world, mimetic desire also creates and spreads fads in groups of people through **mimetic contagion**. The **contagion** moves from person to person and eventually to the entire community. For example, if we look at the fad of body piercing, something that became extremely popular over the past couple of decades, we can see it's become a source of mimetic contagion. Just look at the selection of responses from interviews conducted with individuals ranging from teens to adults with body-piercings. The question asked of the subjects was simply: "Why did you get your body pierced?"[10]

> (A young girl with a nose ring): "Thought it was cool. Had a few friends who had one and I liked how they look on them."
>
> (An undergraduate student with an eyebrow piercing): "Well, I got it when I was dating a girl who had one and I wanted to get the piercing to impress her."
>
> (A girl with two nose rings): "When I got it—it was two years ago—it was the thing to do."

---

9. Flatley, "Why 'A Clockwork Orange' Was Banned," paras. 6–8.
10. The interviews were conducted in 2010 in New York City.

(On lip-piercing and lip-ring): "Well I have ten pierces in my ears ... Then I saw a movie and I liked the lead singer who played in it and I saw the music video, so I thought I'd get one. That's the eleventh."

(On eyebrow piercing): "I saw it in a friend, and I thought it was beautiful, so I got mine pierced. You know there are many countries and cultures in the world that have really beautiful piercing. I think they are beautiful!"

In some of these examples of contagion, nobody really gets hurt because there are plenty of nose rings to go around. Everyone can share the object of desire. Nose rings are in style? I can go and get one too! My having one doesn't take one away from you. In a fad, the object of desire and desire itself may proliferate without doing any real harm.

DESIRE AND CONFLICT: INTERNAL MEDIATION

We saw how external mediation can sometimes turn negative with people copycatting destructive behavior simply because they saw it done by someone else. But such copying behavior can become even more intense when we have a strong mediator nearby the subject. This kind of phenomenon can take on a life of its own. Here, external mediation turns into what Girard calls **internal mediation**—when the subject and the model come close together, in the same social sphere. Let's return to the **mimetic triangle** we drew earlier. We saw how desire is mediated, with the subject imitating the model. With the model far away, their object cannot really be grasped, only sought after generally. But with the model nearby and someone a lot like me, I could actually grasp the things the model desires and strive to become just like them. This leads to what Girard calls mimetic rivalry, as two hands reach for the same object and the subject becomes more and more fascinated with the model.

A fad that begins as relatively harmless external mediation with a distant model for a few may shift into close models and subjects competing intensively for the same object—and the object may achieve a quasi-mythical status like Tom Sawyer's whitewashed fence. This dynamic can be tragic with deadly consequences, creating social, psychological and medical conditions such as anorexia. We can see the mimetic nature of anorexic behavior and widespread rivalry for slimness in the response to the 1960s model and cultural phenomenon known as Twiggy.

What Is Desire?

Twiggy, the first modern supermodel, not only aimed to be as thin as a twig but she garnered a large group of followers amidst young girls who imitated her thin look. (Though boys and men can also have anorexia, it's much less common.) Giving an autobiographical account of her anorexia and her obsession with Twiggy, Marcia Herrin, one of the authors and editors of *The Parent's Guide to Eating Disorders,* tells her own story:

> When I was coming of age in the sixties and early seventies eating disorders were not commonly diagnosed disease as they are today ... But there was the impossibly thin model, Twiggy. ... To young girls like me who were both eager to grow up but anxious about leaving behind the safety of childhood, Twiggy represented our ideal of feminine beauty. The physical attribute that I coveted most was her amazing "no thigh" legs.
>
> It is hard to imagine now what an impact Twiggy had on a generation of teens like me. She was what we aspired to be, and no one questioned the wisdom of that aspiration.[11]

While often people compete only indirectly and generally aspire to be like a distant fashion icon like Twiggy, they also can begin to directly compete with each other. Thus external mediation proves unstable and often becomes internal mediation, creating intense competition between peers. Anorexia tends to be contagious. In his book on *Anorexia*, Girard describes how this social illness first became prominent in the nineteenth century with two aristocratic women, Elizabeth of Austria (wife of Emperor Franz Joseph) nicknamed "Sisi," and her friend Empress Eugenie of France (wife of Napoleon III), who would compete with each other as models for slimness. They started a pattern first among other aristocratic women who copied and competed with them, and then it eventually filtered down to the non-aristocratic classes further away. In a case of anorexia, Girard says, the slimmer a model of beauty or thinness becomes, the more forcefully another will try to keep up: the other becomes a **model-obstacle**. Like Twiggy or the aristocratic Empresses, the model may be at first far away, but the subject's desire becomes increasingly self-destructive if they also have a close friend or friends competing for the same object of desire, a thin body. These kinds of fads or social contagion can literally consume people.

It's almost impossible to see a political, social, or artistic movement arise independent of mimetic desire and the contagion it creates. Mimetic desire becomes particularly strong if it involves close models and

---

11. Herrin and Matsumoto, *Parent's Guide to Eating Disorders,* xvii.

mediators—such as family, friends and colleagues—who serve as immediate models for the subject. Desire spreads from one subject/friend to the other, and soon "plagues" an entire community through rapidly expanding desire and contagious desire for the same object. As we've seen, the object of desire between friends and within a community can be nose rings, the same fashion, a particular college or major, or a particular presidential candidate. If everyone can share the same object there may be copying going on, but there is no rivalry. But often, the specific object becomes less important in these cases as that someone else is doing it, and we want the same thing. As we move into what Girard calls internal mediation we not only want the same thing but we actually begin to desire to become our model *even more* than we want the object they want. In fact, Girard says that what we really want is the "being" of the model, that elusive, something special they seem to possess, even more than the object at hand. Rather than being harmless, Girard calls this type of mimetic internal mediation "rivalrous" desire, because it leads to direct conflict and rivalry between the subject and the model. Its chief characteristic is envy.

A *Sports Illustrated* article at the height of sports icon Michael Jordan's fame in the 1980s discusses various murders that took place as a result of mimetic envy over possession of athletic items, particularly those worn by drug dealers. Michael Eugene Thomas, a 15-year-old admirer of Michael Jordan, was strangled by a 17-year-old basketball friend of his who stole his prized Air Jordan basketball shoes. Although Michael Jordan may have started out as the external mediator for both boys as a distant hero, the presence of the special shoes as an object created envy as the one boy ended up taking the other as a nearby model of desire:

> A ninth grader at Meade Senior High School in Anne Arundel County, Md., Thomas was found strangled on May 2, 1989. Charged with first-degree murder was James David Martin, 17, a basketball buddy who allegedly took Thomas's two-week-old Air Jordan basketball shoes and left Thomas's barefoot body in the woods near school.
>
> Thomas loved Michael Jordan, as well as the shoes Jordan endorses, and he cleaned his own pair each evening. He kept the cardboard shoe box with Jordan's silhouette on it in a place of honor in his room. Inside the box was the sales ticket for the shoes. It showed he paid $115.50; the price of a product touched by deity.[12]

12. Telander, "Senseless," paras 1–2.

What Is Desire?

In this case, the Martin boy not only wanted to take away his friend's shoes, he even replaced his friend turned rival through murder. This was not a singular incident—there were many. The article lists a short history of these types of violent crimes created by mimetic envy starting in 1983 involving additional brands other than the Air Jordan.

Brands prove rife with envy and competition. Internal mediation can be found behind the scenes within families and friends. In fact, two German brothers who hated each other created the shoe brands Puma and Adidas, rivaling each other to such an extent that their rivalry took over their families, their hometown, and was well recognized worldwide. Each wanted the same thing, which was to be admired as the best shoe-brand manufacturer.

Growing up means learning to know the difference between right and wrong. We have good forms of imitation, and then we have bad forms of imitation. We've looked at some of them and have seen how, without proper direction, mimetic desire could lead us astray into destructive forms of behavior. Children, for instance, can be vulnerable to mimetic desire with their peers until they're taught to share. Have you ever seen a situation like this? See what happens if you put young children into a room full of toys. At first, they may not touch any of them. Then one of them picks up a toy and starts playing with it. The rest of the kids may immediately start to cry and want the same exact toy, for no other reason than because another toddler chose it. Although children are also capable from young ages of empathy and sharing, they must be guided by parents about how to desire productively. Unless their parents intervene, competing children will often create a ruckus, as anyone who has taken a car trip with them well knows.

Girard shows how when the subject and model in the mimetic triangle contend for the same object of desire, trouble may follow. As they draw nearer to each other, getting too close for comfort to each other so the subject begins to desire the very same object the model has *and that object cannot be shared*, rivalry may set in, and conflict will result. You may even have violence.

Where does violence come from? How does it work? Why do we hurt each other, even kill each other, and how does this relate to mimetic desire? We'll talk more about these questions in the following chapters.

FOR REFLECTION

Now before we move on, let's apply what we've learned in this first chapter.

- Think back to an occasion when you desired a certain fashion. Why did you follow that fashion? Were you copying somebody else? Who do you think you were you imitating?
- Think back to a time when you were jealous of someone. Or remember when you were a rival of another person. What were your thoughts and feelings? What were your desires?
- Think back to your youth—high school, for example. Remember the time when you first fell in love. What made you desire the other person? Was anyone else in love with that person, too? Did their love for that person affect your feelings for that person?

2

Doubles and the Mimetic Crisis

As we saw in the previous chapter, desire, which Girard calls mimetic desire, can be both a positive force or a destructive one. We've talked about external mediation, where the subject and model are far from each other so there's no rivalry over the model's desired objects. We've started to look at the dynamic of internal mediation and see how it can lead to a full-blown crisis by creating rivalry, envy, and violence. But how does this crisis begin? In this chapter we'll look at some examples from literary works to see how the dynamic of mimetic desire in internal mediation works and can become deadly.

Our previous examples about something as simple as Michael Jordan sneakers demonstrate how, through an escalation of the mimetic crisis, desire becomes envy. **Envy** can be defined as simply "desiring what others have and not being able to obtain it." Looking at envy as one side of a coin, the flip side would be rivalry. **Rivalry** describes the state of conflict or competition between a subject and model over possession of the exact same object that cannot be shared between them.

As we've seen in the previous chapter, when the subject can attain the object the model wants without undermining the model; when the object stays out of reach for the subject; or when the distance between the subject and model remains great enough, the mimetic crisis is kept at bay. The triangle of desire remains at a level of external mediation. But when the model becomes a target of envy with the model nearby, then the subject's approach, perspective, and psychology can easily shift into internal mediation—a rivalry-based competition. The competition only gets more competitive and fiercer if, like a stone wall, the model deflects the subject's attempts to win the contest. Here, in this form of mimetic desire, the model becomes a **model-obstacle**. No matter how hard the subject tries to imitate the model, the model acts like a rejection machine, becoming an obstacle in the path of the subject.

Ironically, as the mimetic crisis increases, the object of desire decreases in importance. It practically disappears! Why? Because the subject's desire becomes fully focused on the other person, the model, the mediator. Girard calls this **metaphysical desire**, because the subject really begins to desire not just the model's objects, but something elusive about the model's being itself. The subject wants some kind of intangible prestige they perceive the model as having, and they may even want to *become* the model! (We will discuss this more in the next chapter as well.) Mimetic energy reverberates back from the model to the subject. They are caught in a process known as **double mediation** as they imitate one another's desire.[1]

Figure 2: double mediation

In an infinite mirroring or a feedback loop, the model and subject become endlessly focused on one another. The more desire mirrors back and forth between the two, the more rapidly it will oscillate. This leads to the eventual breakdown of all distinctions and differences between the two parties: they begin to resemble one another, and their desires also become indistinguishable. To resolve the growing crisis, either something must reintroduce differentiation between the two, or one of the two must yield to return matters to normality.

Girard shows us how **mimetic doubling,** where the subject and the model imitate and rival each other for the object at hand, can oscillate so

---

1. In certain cases, the model encourages the subject to imitate him or her, but then upon the start of imitation, intervenes and stops the subject from imitating. This phenomenon, referred to as the *double bind,* was first discovered and articulated by Gregory Bateson in "Toward a Theory of Schizophrenia," "Minimal Requirements for a Theory of Schizophrenia," and "Double Bind, 1969" in Bateson, et al., *Steps to an Ecology of Mind.*

fast and so rapidly that it cannot be stopped, turning each person into identical images or **doubles** of the other (even though they may deny this is happening and insist that they are nothing like their "enemy"). Think of the twentieth-century Cold War between the US and the USSR of that time, with each accusing the other of being the enemy of civilization and escalating a deadly competition for the possession of the most nuclear warheads. The two superpowers became obsessed with one another and engaged in similar language and actions toward each other, all while emphasizing how they were completely different. This competition brought the superpowers to the brink of a new level of war. They became doubles. Doubling can be found between sons and fathers, daughters and mothers, students and teachers, between friends, or even between nations and politicians! Let's look at some good examples of doubling in famous literary works.

PSYCHOLOGY OF THE MIMETIC CRISIS

We'll be looking at Shakespeare as the arch-playwright who understands human nature and can express insights through poetry, dynamic metaphors, and clever plots. But first let's look at the modern American playwright Eugene O'Neill for an example of mimetic rivalry and doubling between two brothers. Here we find a twentieth-century psychological portrayal of the mimetic phenomenon in its essence. O'Neill's first play, *Beyond the Horizon* (1920), uses what we call the construct of doubles as a central dramatic mechanism of conflict. Our doubles are the Mayo brothers, Andrew and Robert. As we will see, a mimetic crisis unfolds when Robert (the subject) desires something that Andrew (the model) has that cannot be shared—a relationship with Ruth, a young woman.

The brothers at first seem opposites of one another, in both their physical build and personality. The stark contrast suggests a peaceful complementarity: Andrew is a practical, sun-bronzed "son of the soil" who enjoys working "the good clean earth" and Robert a daydreaming, sensitive young poet. The distance between the two brothers and their respective objects of desire seems wide: Robert has his poetry and daydreams of the world beyond the horizon, while Andrew is content with the farm, the soil, his home, and his family. They maintain their distance through mutual respect for one another's spheres. Their banter about the soil—it is both "dirt" and "good clean earth"—manifests gentle brotherhood and respect.

Looking at the earth for a moment, the brothers imagine their roles reversed, with Andrew reading poems from a journal and Robert plowing the field. Quickly, they abandon the thought. Andrew isn't fit to be the scholar. Robert, with a laugh, admits he's not fit to plow the field. Andrew suddenly stops joking and adopts a sober tone of voice. He acknowledges some health difficulties Robert has had and endorses his brother's desire to be in school and learn: "You should have gone back to college last fall, like I know you wanted to. You're fitted for that sort of thing—just as I ain't."[2] Robert gives his reason for not having gone back: their father needed the money for improving the farm. To this Robert adds that he's had enough of school and was looking forward to sailing in his uncle's ship and seeing the world—India, Australia, South Africa, or South America. Andrew again creates distance with his response: "You can have all those foreign parts for all of me."[3] The two brothers seem like night and day. Nothing appears to attract these opposites.

In the scene, Andrew suddenly jumps off the fence, remarking that he'd "better run along." He remarks: "I've got to wash up some as long as Ruth's Ma is coming over for dinner."[4] The mood shifts. Robert adds "(*pointedly—almost bitterly*) And Ruth." Everything passing between the brothers thus far has avoided a taboo subject. But Robert names it. A tension arises. Andrew looks away from Robert and tries to deflate the situation: "Yes, Ruth'll be staying too."[5] As if Andrew himself was not the only reason for Ruth Atkins's visit, he adds Ruth's mother as well. We can see that Andrew tries here to deflect attention from himself, making Ruth instead the person of brothers' mutual object of desire. He also tries to make Ruth the object of *everyone's* desire by saying that Ruth isn't really Andrew's guest; she's just a guest of the Mayo family. Andrew has defused the tension—for now; but Robert, triggered by thoughts of Ruth, finds his desire inflamed.

We have here the beginning of rivalry and a mimetic crisis. Let's examine how this example of internal mediation works out. O'Neill describes Robert's frame of mind as someone "who appears to be fighting some strong inward emotion—impulsively." Robert struggles with his impermissible desire for Ruth, modeled by his brother. His desire for Ruth is further heightened by the fact that within days he'll be sailing away, sealing

---

2. O'Neill, *Complete Plays 1913–1920*, 574.
3. O'Neill, *Complete Plays 1913–1920*, 575.
4. O'Neill, *Complete Plays 1913–1920*, 577.
5. O'Neill, *Complete Plays 1913–1920*, 577.

DOUBLES AND THE MIMETIC CRISIS

the impossibility of obtaining her love. He wishes to speak of his desire to Andrew, but he fails. Robert backs down and the die is cast. Like cowboys in a showdown, in a pivotal scene we have the image of two brothers facing one another, eye to eye, the perfect dramatic icon for doubles. They fixate on each other and become like each other. Ruth and the Mayo brothers have found themselves in a triangle of mimetic desire with Ruth as the object. The dynamics between Ruth, Andrew, and Robert are as clear to Ruth as they are to the Mayo brothers, though the brothers lack the courage to acknowledge it.

Next the play gives us a dramatic turnabout: the role reversal casually rejected by the Mayo brothers actually happens. Robert and Andrew swap desires. Robert, the poet, remains on the farm, works the land, and ends up raising a family with Ruth. Andrew, the "son of the soil," looking upon Robert and Ruth with envy, takes his brother's place on his uncle's boat and travels the world far away from the farm.

Beyond the Horizon gives us O'Neill's earliest use of what we call mimetic doubles. But he was far from the first to employ them as the dynamic core of the genre of tragedy. The rivalry of brothers is a very common pattern in dramatic literature. Witness the story of Cain and Abel in Genesis, the first book of the Bible, to which we will turn later; or the story of the murder of Remus by Romulus at the founding of Rome. How quickly the peaceful pastoral landscape of "rolling hills and freshly plowed field" can become a field of blood! In mythology and dramatic literature, competing brothers have often been the image for the mimetic crisis leading to the formation of rivalrous doubles, whose conflict cannot seem to resolve until one or the other is killed, sacrificed, or dies.

COWBOYS IN SHOWDOWN

Here's another example of doubling between brothers in modern drama. In this play, the rivalrous object of desire proves to be not a love interest but a profession and identity. In *True West* written by Sam Shepard in 1981, the protagonists, Lee and Austin, start off as brothers with nothing in common on the surface. Austin is an Ivy League–educated, well-dressed screenwriter in his early thirties. Lee is an unkempt drifter in his early forties. The play opens with Austin house-sitting for his mother while working on a screenplay and Lee "mildly drunk" sipping on beer. The scene brims with tension. Austin tries to write, but he finds himself being constantly interrupted by Lee, who shows resentment and an inferiority complex. He also taunts Austin about being a snob about being a writer; in contrast, Lee, passing through the neighborhood, plans on stealing "electric devices." He asks to borrow Austin's car. Reluctant to give Lee his keys, Austin says he has a film producer stopping by later in the afternoon to discuss a project. They reach a resolution when Austin lets Lee have his car until the evening.

Austin meets with Saul Kimmer, the producer, and it goes over well. Just as they conclude, Lee arrives with a stolen television. In front of Saul, he lies that the television belongs to Austin and he's just brought it back from the repair shop. He remarks he can now watch the amateur boxing—but Lee's remark gives us a double entendre, foreshadowing the sparring of the brothers between themselves. Austin tries to usher Saul out of the house, but Lee intervenes, blocking their way. He has a pitch to make:

> Lee: I got a Western that'd knock yer lights out.
>
> Saul: Oh really?
>
> Lee: Yeah. Contemporary Western. Based on a true story. 'Course I'm not like my brother here. I'm not a man of the pen.[6]

The scene ends with Lee promising to call Saul the next day for a game of golf. Austin demands his car keys back, but Lee "doesn't move, just stares at Austin, smiles," and the lights fade to black.

The next scene reveals Austin behind the typewriter, typing an outline for Lee's impromptu film proposal as a ransom for his car keys. Tossing the car keys on the table, Lee gives an ultimatum: Austin can call the police, because it's the only way he can remove him. To this Austin responds: "You're my brother."[7] Lee says: "That don't mean a thing. You go down to the L.A. Police Department there and ask them what kinda' people kill each other the most. What do you think they'd say?"[8] Austin: "Who said anything about killing?" Lee: "Family people. Brothers. Brothers-in-law. Cousins. Real American-type people. They kill each other in the heat mostly. . . . Right about this time a year."[9] Austin rationalizes that the two of them are educated and different and would know better. He says he'd be happy to write the screenplay outline for Lee: "No, really, look, I'll write it out for

---

6. Shepard, *Seven Plays*, 18.
7. Shepard, *Seven Plays*, 23.
8. Shepard, *Seven Plays*, 23.
9. Shepard, *Seven Plays*, 24.

Doubles and the Mimetic Crisis

you. I think it's a great idea."[10] Without letting Lee change the subject, Austin insists:

> Austin: Why don't we try to see this through, Lee. Just for the hell of it. Maybe you've really got something here. What do you think?
>
> Lee: Maybe so. No harm in tryin' I guess. You think it's such a hot idea. Besides, I always wondered what'd be like to be you.
>
> Austin: You did?
>
> Lee: Yeah sure. I used to picture you walkin' around some campus with yer arms fulla' books. Blonds chasin' after ya'.
>
> Austin: Blonds? That's funny.
>
> Lee: What's funny about it?
>
> Austin: Because I always used to picture you somewhere.
>
> Lee: Where'd you picture me?
>
> Austin: Oh, I don't know. Different places. Adventures. You were always on some adventure.
>
> Lee: Yeah.
>
> Austin: And I used to say to myself, "Lee's got the right idea. He's out there in the world and here I am. What am I doing?"[11]

These brothers tread on dangerous ground. Each wants to have what the other has. Lee fantasizes about the lifestyle of Austin the collegian; Austin seeks the freedom and adventure he imagines in Lee. Their desires converge around the film script Lee has proposed. With promises of good fortune, the scene ends with Lee dictating the outline and Austin typing it out. The brothers have been reborn as doubles. What had appeared to be a big difference between brothers starts to explode into similarity and conflict. The situation grows more unstable as the identities of Austin and Lee dissolve and melt into one another.

Having lost a bet over a game of golf to Lee, Saul now agrees to drop Austin's script and pick up Lee's instead. This doesn't settle well with Austin. He can't reach Saul and he tries to talk sense with Lee: his livelihood is at stake. When Austin refuses to share details of his own script with Lee, it triggers his brother: "Ha! 'Fraid I'll steal it huh? Competition's getting' kinda'

---

10. Shepard, *Seven Plays*, 24.
11. Shepard, *Seven Plays*, 26.

close to home isn't it?"[12] Austin now says the new outline belongs to himself—Lee does not have the right to be "peddling it around." Nevertheless, Austin has the weaker hand. Saul reappears, this time as Lee's partner, and together they try to convince Austin to write Lee's screenplay for him. The brothers have experienced a complete reversal of fortune. When the lights come up next, Lee types with one finger while Austin, drunk on whiskey, sits on the kitchen floor. Austin sings and mocks him: "You are going to write an entire script on your own?" Lee responds: "That's right."[13] Austin remarks of Saul, "He thinks we're the same person." Austin may be more right than he knows, because the brothers have become doubles. Saul mistakenly believes both brothers can write. Lee boasts: "I'm a screenwriter now! I'm legitimate." Laughing at his usurping brother, Austin wonders aloud: "Well, maybe I outa' go out and try my hand at your trade. Since you are doing so good at mine."[14] Lee taunts Austin: "You couldn't steal a toaster without losin' yer lunch."[15] Austin responds, "You don't think I could sneak into somebody's house and steal a toaster?"[16] The boasting becomes a reality: Lee continues the screenplay while Austin goes out and steals toasters at night. In the next scene, Lee smashes the typewriter with a golf club while Austin polishes his trove of stolen toasters. Each brother inhabits the other's former identity and the doubling becomes complete. In a climactic scene, Lee becomes ever more predatory and explosive: he says that if Austin finishes the script just as he says and gives him all the credits and all the rights, Lee will take him to the desert. Austin agrees to this "deal." Austin desires Lee's street-smarts, know-how, and desert lifestyle, while Lee wants Austin's worldly success, power, and control. More than this, each brother wants to *be* the other. In the process of mimetic doubling, each man takes the other as the model as desire oscillates back and forth between the two. In these close quarters, the friction gets high, the rivalry fierce. With their desires left unchecked, where will these doubles go from here? What's their end?

In the final scene, the crisis resumes when Lee breaks his promise and decides to go to the desert without Austin. In response, Austin takes a phone cord and wraps it around Lee's neck while demanding his car keys, continuing to hold the telephone cord tightly. Lee thrashes while Austin

---

12. Shepard, *Seven Plays*, 32.
13. Shepard, *Seven Plays*, 36.
14. Shepard, *Seven Plays*, 37.
15. Shepard, *Seven Plays*, 37.
16. Shepard, *Seven Plays*, 37.

subdues him with the cord; he becomes motionless and appears to be dead. But just as Austin makes for his exit, Lee jumps to his feet, squaring off with his brother and blocking the way out. The final image of the play shows a silhouette of a trapped pair. The stage directions say, "the figures of the brothers now appear to be caught in a vast desert-like landscape, they are very still but watchful for the next move, lights go slowly to black as the after-image of the brothers pulses in the dark, coyote fades."[17] *True West* illustrates the mimetic crisis as a recurring cycle of doubling and violence between enemy brothers without resolution. This type of doubling often appears in tragic plots.

METAPHYSICAL DESIRE

Through these examples of modern literature, we've seen how the mimetic crisis leads from an external mediation—the subject desires the object the model desires but cannot attain it—to an internal mediation—the subject actually starts to desire the model's immediate object, or even eventually to become the model. This movement into internal mediation describes the phenomenon we call metaphysical desire, which is desire not just for the model's object *per se* but for the model's own qualities—to actually be what they are. The consequences of unchecked metaphysical desire and the doubling that ensues can be deadly. We can see this dynamic again in Peter Shaffer's play, *Amadeus,* which in 1984 was made into an Academy-Award winning movie. The story involves the court composer, Antonio Salieri (the subject), who covets the great genius of Wolfgang Amadeus Mozart (the model). Salieri fiercely desires Mozart's preeminence: he's obsessed with Mozart. He will stop at nothing and pay any price to capture Mozart's talent for himself. He not only wants Mozart's talent and fame through mimetic rivalry, but he also actually wants to *become* him. Salieri's desire for the prestige or fame of the model, that certain something the model has, is intangible and all consuming.

The play begins in Vienna, November 1823. We start with a mystery: was Mozart murdered by Salieri, or did he die of natural causes? The play flashes back to 1781 to let us know the twenty-five-year-old Mozart has come to Salzburg. Here, Salieri provides us a possible motive as he confesses: "As for your Mozart, I confess I was alarmed by his coming. Not by the commission of a comic opera, even though I myself was then attempting

17. Shepard, *Seven Plays,* 59.

one called *The Stolen Buckett*.... No, what worried me were reports about the man himself. He was praised altogether too much."[18]

Mozart's arrival not only alarms Salieri but simply listening to his music throws him into physical pain! Listening to Mozart's performance of an *adagio* sends Salieri into a fit: "Ah, the pain! Pain as I had never known it."[19] While pretending to be Mozart's friend and patron, Salieri undertakes secret warfare, undermining Mozart at every possible occasion. Mozart never suspects the sabotage, while Salieri effectively reduces Mozart to a life of poverty and exposes him to ridicule in the court of the emperor.

In one scene we witness Constanze, Mozart's wife, going to Salieri's apartment with Mozart's compositions to gain an endorsement:

> Constanze: ... I brought you some manuscripts by Wolfgang. When you see them, you'll understand how right he is for royal appointment. Will you look at them, please, while I wait?[20]

But Constanze comes to see that Salieri isn't the benign patron and professional friend Salieri pretends to be. Without a job or commission and ill, Mozart tries to tell Constanze of his nightmares he has each night, but unsympathetic, she refuses to listen:

> Mozart: I'm frightened Stanzi.... Something aweful's happening to me. The pains stay. And the dreams!...
>
> Constanze: [*Quietly*] I can't bear it. I can't bear much more of this.
>
> Mozart: The Figure's like this now—[*Beckoning more urgently*]— Here. Come here... It's face still hidden. Always hidden.
>
> Constanze: [*Crying out*]. Stop it, for God sake's stop it!... Stop it ... Stop ... It's me who is frightened ... *Me!* ... You frighten me ... If you go on like this I will leave you. I swear it.
>
> Mozart:[Shocked] Stanzi!
>
> Constanze: I mean it ... I do ...[21]

The scene does not tell us what the pains are all about, just that they are psychological as well as physical pains. Mozart starts recounting his pain to his wife, then she picks up and continues with hers. Could it be a state of mimetic doubling where Constanze, not knowing what to do or how to

18. Shaffer, *Amadeus*, 23.
19. Shaffer, *Amadeus*, 27.
20. Shaffer, *Amadeus*, 53.
21. Shaffer, *Amadeus*, 94.

respond to her husband, is imitating Mozart? The tension and bewilderment between the two dies out when Mozart apologizes and "kneels and coaxes her to him" and Constanze "half-unreluctantly, half-willing" goes to Mozart. She finally "surrenders" and they play a game with one other:

> Constanze: Wolfi-polfi!
>
> Mozart: Poopy-peepee!
>
> [They giggle.][22]

While like children they "rub noses" and have a good time, suddenly Constance "cries out in distress, and clutches her stomach."[23] Salieri walks on stage and explains: "And suddenly she was delivered! A boy!"[24] During the scene, Constanze "has slowly risen, divested herself of her stuffed apron—thereby ceasing to be pregnant. Now she turns sorrowfully and walks briskly upstage and off it. Mozart follows her for a few steps, alarmed. He halts."[25] With Constanze and the boy going off the stage and Mozart, not joining them but halting on stage, visually and theatrically demonstrating the characters now being in different spaces. This becomes clear later in the scene when Mozart and Salieri have a discussion:

> Mozart: Constanze's gone away. Just for a while, she says. She's taken the baby and gone to Baden. To the spa. It'll cost us the last money that we had.
>
> Salieri: But *why*?
>
> Mozart: [Distressed] She's right to go! It's my fault! She thinks I'm mad.[26]

Having heard about Mozart's madness, Salieri sets out to Mozart's apartment to witness it with his own eyes. Salieri plays a friend and assures Mozart that he is not mad. Mozart on the other hand insists that what he saw and heard was real:

> Mozart: I was seated at my table working. Suddenly there came three sharp knocks at the door, and a Figure entered, all muffled in grey. But now it had a *face! A death's-head!*—glaring at me with frozen eyes sunk deep in little caves of bone . . . And then it *spoke!*

22. Shaffer, *Amadeus*, 94–95.
23. Shaffer, *Amadeus*, 95.
24. Shaffer, *Amadeus*, 95.
25. Shaffer, *Amadeus*, 95.
26. Shaffer, *Amadeus*, 96.

A horrible sound like a man hissing ... It said, "Wolfgang Mozart: you are required now by my master to write Requiem Mass. ... It must be finished completely when you see me next. And tell no one." I asked, "Who has died? Who is this Requiem for? ... And who is your Master?"[27]

Taking pride in Mozart's loss and misery, Salieri remarks, "I couldn't have managed it myself."[28]

Salieri's stratagem "design[s] to hasten him towards madness, or towards death." Mozart, driven to exhaustion, finishes the composition without recompense and without discovering the identity of the patron. Constanze and their son return only to find Mozart on his deathbed, ready to breath his last breath: "Can you hear me? ... You've got to get well, Wolfi—because we need you. Karl and Baby Franz as well. There's only the three of us: we don't cost much."[29] Meanwhile, Salieri, victorious over Mozart, has failed to attain the greatness (the object, the being) of his rival. He resigns himself to the fate of obscurity: "Now I go to become a ghost myself. ... I will whisper my name: Salieri—Patron Saint of Mediocrities."[30] Salieri has been consumed by metaphysical desire in mimetic doubling until both he and his model/rival are vanquished. Rivalry for an intangible object has burnt itself out in death.

Doubling, and the escalation into extreme doubles caused by internal mediation and metaphysical desire, initiates the first phase of the mimetic crisis. If it doesn't get resolved soon, it gets worse. The doubles can multiply beyond the initial triangle. Much like an epidemic, mimetic desire can infect others and spread like a virus into the community and the society. How can we observe this phenomenon safely, from a distance? Fiction gives us a way to see ourselves.

Let's go to William Shakespeare, who understands humanity so well. In *A Midsummer Night's Dream* Hermia exclaims in frustration, "O hell! to choose love by another's eyes" (I.i.140). We couldn't ask for a more concise definition of mimetic desire! Shakespeare wasn't a psychologist or a social scientist. He lived 400 years before René Girard introduced mimetic desire. But as a poet, playwright, and "man of theatre," he was intuitively aware of the mechanisms of desire. He employed them to drive the plots in many

27. Shaffer, *Amadeus*, 96.
28. Shaffer, *Amadeus*, 101.
29. Shaffer, *Amadeus*, 112.
30. Shaffer, *Amadeus*, 117.

DOUBLES AND THE MIMETIC CRISIS

of his plays and to create conflicts between his characters. What could be more dramatic, funny, or tragic than watching two people fall in love with the same person? In his comedies such as *A Midsummer Night's Dream* Shakespeare shows us how desire works within a group of friends. We want what the other person wants. We can copy the other individual so well that before we know it, we become their double, entering into rivalry and envy. Our unthinking imitation of others, especially close friends, gives rise to complications and often serious conflicts.

MIMETIC DESIRE AND A WEB OF DOUBLING

In his much-loved and often staged comedy, *A Midsummer Night's Dream*, Shakespeare uses mimetic desire to show us the foibles of a set of people romantically entangled. We have two pairs of doubles, two women and two men, each pair the victim of the other pair's desires, masked under the guise of "love." The rivalry within the sexes for who is in love with whom ensnares the protagonists into a complex web of mimetic doubling, creating a comedy with rather cruel and vicious overtones, in which mimetic desire spreads itself to the whole community. Only by outside intervention does the plot resolve peacefully.

The play opens in the palace of Duke Theseus, with a conflict between a daughter, Hermia, and her father Eugeus. Hermia loves Lysander, but her father wants her to marry Demetrius. He wants Hermia to see and understand matters through *her father's eyes* and to prefer Demetrius as he does. Hermia turns the tables: why can't her father see things as she does? Right from the first scene of the comedy, we see the conflict of desire—Hermia's desire to be the model and her father's desire for the same makes them at odds but also similar. Refusing to wed Demetrius, Hermia receives an ultimatum from Duke Theseus: "Either to die the death, or abjure/For ever the society of men."[31] Her suitor Lysander enters the scene in defense of his love for Hermia, presenting himself an equal to Demetrius: his presentation to the duke leaves little doubt he's a rival to be reckoned with. Demetrius and Egeus exit with the duke, while Lysander and Hermia lament the traps of desire, the slavish imitation of another's bidding, with Hermia here exclaiming "O hell! To choose love by another's eyes" (the theme which will run throughout the play). Wishing to escape the traps laid out by Egeus

---

31. Shakespeare, *Midsummer Night's Dream*, I.i.65–66.

and Duke Theseus, the lovers decide to meet in the woods the next night to escape the Athenian law and to take refuge with Lysander's aunt.

With the promise and plan sealed, our other female protagonist Helena enters the scene. Immediately the exchange between the female protagonists sets the stage for their rivalry:

> Hermia: God speed fair Helena! whither away?
>
> Helena: Call you me fair? that fair again unsay.
> Demetrius loves your fair: O happy fair!
> Your eyes are lode-stars; and your tongue's sweet air
> More tuneable than lark to shepherd's ear,
> When wheat is green, when hawthorn buds appear.[32]

What follows is Helena's open confession of desire to be like Hermia.

> Helena: Sickness is catching: O, were favour so,
> Yours would I catch, fair Hermia, ere I go;
> My ear should catch your voice, my eye your eye,
> My tongue should catch your tongue's sweet melody.
> Were the world mine, Demetrius being bated,
> The rest I'd give to be to you translated.[33]

Helena seeks from Hermia her secrets of desire: "O, teach me how you look, and with what art/You sway the motion of Demetrius' heart."[34] She wants to become like Hermia so Demetrius will love her. Not knowing how to respond, Hermia speaks only what she knows has been working with Demetrius: igniting desire simply by denouncing it and rejecting him. The exchange between the two becomes rapid, with Helena wishing more and more to be like Hermia:

> Hermia: I frown upon him, yet he loves me still.
>
> Helena: O that your frowns would teach my smiles such skill!
>
> Hermia: I give him curses, yet he gives me love.
>
> Helena: O that my prayers could such affection move!
>
> Hermia: The more I hate, the more he follows me.
>
> Helena: The more I love, the more he hateth me.
>
> Hermia: His folly, Helena, is no fault of mine.

---

32. Shakespeare, *Midsummer Night's Dream*, I.i.180–85.
33. Shakespeare, *Midsummer Night's Dream* I.i.186–91.
34. Shakespeare, *Midsummer Night's Dream* I.i.192–93.

> Helena: None, but your beauty: would that fault were mine![35]

Attempting to quench Helena's desire, Hermia and Lysander disclose their plan to flee Athens the following night. The news only adds fuel to Helena's envy. She decides to betray their plans to Demetrius.

The following night in the woods, Helena pursues Demetrius. He rejects her: "I love thee not, therefore pursue me not"[36] and "Do I entice you? do I speak you fair?/Or, rather, do I not in plainest truth/Tell you, I do not, nor I cannot love you?"[37] Demetrius's rejection only inflames Helena's desire. She's even willing to go as far as to be treated like Demetrius's dog. But the more Demetrius rejects Helena's desire for him, the more Helena desires him.

> Demetrius: Tempt not too much the hatred of my spirit; For I am sick when I do look on thee.
>
> Helena: And I am sick when I look not on you.[38]

Intrigue intensifies in the woods. Lysander and Hermia have fallen asleep, and Helena comes running after Demetrius. Adding to the mischief, Puck, a fairy, squeezes a potion upon the eyes of Lysander so that upon waking, he'll fall in love with the first person he sees. Helena, in hot pursuit of Demetrius, is consumed with envy of her model, her double, Hermia: "The more my prayer, the lesser my grace. / Happy is Hermia, wheresoe'er she lie; / For she hath blessed and attractive eyes."[39] Awakening, Lysander sees Helena running through the woods, and under the spell of the potion instantly falls in love with her: "Content with Hermia! No: I do repent / The tedious minutes I with her have spent./ Not Hermia, but Helena I love: / Who will not change a raven for a dove?"[40] At the end of Act II, Hermia, now alone in the woods, awakens from a nightmare: "Help me, Lysander, help me! Do thy best / To pluck this crawling serpent from my breast!"[41] She sets out in the forest alone, stating that she will either find Lysander or death immediately.

---

35. Shakespeare, *Midsummer Night's Dream* I.i.194–201.
36. Shakespeare, *Midsummer Night's Dream* II.i.188.
37. Shakespeare, *Midsummer Night's Dream* II.i.199–201.
38. Shakespeare, *Midsummer Night's Dream* II.i.211–13.
39. Shakespeare, *Midsummer Night's Dream* II.ii.89–91.
40. Shakespeare, *Midsummer Night's Dream* II.ii.111–14.
41. Shakespeare, *Midsummer Night's Dream* II.ii.145–46.

How Violence Works

In Act III Scene ii, we find Demetrius and Hermia leveling violent accusations against one another.

> Demetrius: O, why rebuke you him that loves you so?
> Lay breath so bitter on your bitter foe.
>
> Hermia: Now I but chide; but I should use thee worse,
> For thou, I fear, hast given me cause to curse,
> If thou hast slain Lysander in his sleep,
> Being o'er shoes in blood, plunge in the deep,
> And kill me too.[42]

Meanwhile, Lysander expresses his new love to Helena. She's incredulous—no matter what he does or says, Helena won't accept it. Helena mistrusts Lysander as much as she envies Hermia and no matter how honest Lysander tries to be, Helena rejects him: "These vows are Hermia's: will you give her o'er?"[43] Lysander, in his self-defense, can now only conjure up his double, Demetrius: "Demetrius loves her [Hermia], and he loves not you."[44]

Now comes the clever twist in the plot: Puck also awakens Demetrius with the love potion, and his flooded eyes set sights on Helena, who he has previously rejected. Now he professes:

> Demetrius: O Helena, goddess, nymph, perfect, divine!
> To what, my love, shall I compare thine eyne?
> Crystal is muddy. O, how ripe in show
> Thy lips, those kissing cherries, tempting grow!
> That pure congealed white, high Taurus snow,
> Fann'd with the eastern wind, turns to a crow
> When thou hold'st up thy hand: O, let me kiss
> This princess of pure white, this seal of bliss![45]

Helena, seeing the doubling and rivalry between the two men (but blind to her own), chastises them both for what looks to her like mockery.

> Helena: O spite! O hell! I see you all are bent
> To set against me for your merriment:
> If you were civil and knew courtesy,
> You would not do me thus much injury.[46]

---

42. Shakespeare, *Midsummer Night's Dream* III.ii.43–49.
43. Shakespeare, *Midsummer Night's Dream* III.ii.130.
44. Shakespeare, *Midsummer Night's Dream* III.ii.136.
45. Shakespeare, *Midsummer Night's Dream* III.ii.137–44.
46. Shakespeare, *Midsummer Night's Dream* III.ii.145–48.

Doubles and the Mimetic Crisis

> Helena: Can you not hate me, as I know you do,
> But you must join in souls to mock me too?
> If you were men, as men you are in show,
> You would not use a gentle lady so;
> To vow, and swear, and superpraise my parts,
> When I am sure you hate me with your hearts.
> You both are rivals, and love Hermia;
> And now both rivals, to mock Helena.[47]

Next comes the bargaining of the doubles, where Lysander and Demetrius each ask the other to give up his love for Helena and live content with Hermia instead. To complicate matters, Hermia enters the scene. She believes that nothing has changed and that Lysander loves her as he did before. She proclaims her love aloud: "What love could press Lysander from my side?" but he answers her:

> Lysander: Lysander's love, that would not let him bide,
> Fair Helena, who more engilds the night
> Than all you fiery O's and eyes of light.
> Why seek'st thou me? could not this make thee know,
> The hate I bear thee made me leave thee so?
>
> Hermia: You speak not as you think: it cannot be.[48]

Hearing of Hermia's love for Lysander despite his rejection of her, Helena rushes to judgment—she thinks it must be a conspiracy of the three lovers against her: "Now I perceive they have conjoin'd all three/To fashion this false sport, in spite of me."[49] Not being able to truly understand the doubling between herself and her schoolfriend, Helena appeals to Hermia's friendship. Her description of the two friends paints us a paragon of doubles:

> Helena: All school-days' friendship, childhood innocence?
> We, Hermia, like two artificial gods,
> Have with our needles created both one flower,
> Both on one sampler, sitting on one cushion,
> Both warbling of one song, both in one key,
> As if our hands, our sides, voices and minds,
> Had been incorporate. So we grow together,
> Like to a double cherry, seeming parted,

---

47. Shakespeare, *Midsummer Night's Dream* III.ii.149–56.
48. Shakespeare, *Midsummer Night's Dream* III.ii.186–91.
49. Shakespeare, *Midsummer Night's Dream* III.ii.193–94.

> But yet an union in partition;
> Two lovely berries moulded on one stem;
> So, with two seeming bodies, but one heart;
> Two of the first, like coats in heraldry,
> Due but to one and crowned with one crest.[50]

She presses Hermia for the cause of such mockery: "And will you rent our ancient love asunder, / To join with men in scorning your poor friend? / It is not friendly, 'tis not maidenly. . . ."[51] The relationship within these pairs of doubles, both the men and women, further disintegrates as Demetrius and Lysander continue to vie in rivalry for Helena, and Helena and Hermia start to scorn one another. Between the sexes, Lysander spurns his previous lover Hermia's love. Helena sees a mortal threat in Hermia for Demetrius's love. Desires circulate and escalate between the characters without resolution. For the audience all this is very funny, but also very ominous.

At last, Helena confesses to Hermia that she told Demetrius of Hermia and Lysander's secret flight into the woods and followed him. Reckoning with these foolish adventures, she now wishes to return to Athens: "And follow you no further: let me go: You see how simple and how fond I am."[52] Meanwhile, the two men, blinded by rivalry, speak in defense of Helena against Hermia.

Will these lovers ever be set free from their web? The increasing rivalry needs a solution from outside at this point. The play gives us one: They all fall asleep in the woods, and Puck makes his rounds with the magic potion once again. The next time we see the lovers together it's at the duke's palace in Athens. The doubles have disappeared; things have now fallen into their proper place for the peaceful resolution of the plot. Demetrius now loves Helena, and Lysander once again loves Hermia. Remarking on the night before, Hermia observes: "Methinks I see these things with parted eye,/When everything seems double."[53] Puck, the troublemaker behind it all, gives a final conciliatory speech to the audience, saying all is well and asking forgiveness for his mischief, saying that all the trouble was only a dream.

A happy ending, right? No one has died; this is comedy, not tragedy. But Puck's apologies can't conceal the latent psychological and even

---

50. Shakespeare, *Midsummer Night's Dream* III.ii.202–14.
51. Shakespeare, *Midsummer Night's Dream* III.ii.215–17.
52. Shakespeare, *Midsummer Night's Dream* III.ii.316–17.
53. Shakespeare, *Midsummer Night's Dream* IV.i.195–96.

physical violence intimated throughout most of the play. We're mistaken to see *A Midsummer Night's Dream* merely as a light comedy. A close examination of Shakespeare's language, in particular the dialogue between the lover-doubles, reveals elements of envy, rivalry and doubling whose potential for destruction we see vividly revealed in Shakespeare's other plays such as tragedies like *Macbeth, King Lear,* or *Julius Caesar.*

Mimetic desire catalyzes the plots of great literature. Shakespeare's romantic comedies teach us about human nature. We fall in love so easily. We fall in love by hearsay. We fall in love with the person our close friend loves. You may protest that Shakespearean love triangles don't exist in real life. These are fantasies, nothing but fiction, right? But then why does Shakespeare have such a reputation for understanding human nature, and why have his plays lasted so long? We still perform them today, and laugh and cry at their tangled plots. Maybe he's getting at something we recognize in everyday life. Each of us participates in a great number of triangles of desire. We're never not a part of them in some form, benign or rivalrous. Just as gravity always exerts its force upon us, so do the mechanisms of desire. We may not be conscious of them, but they're at work in us. Literature can help us see these patterns to which we may be blind, and into which great writers may have special insight.

From love triangles to struggles for political power, you can find the mechanism of desire at work everywhere in literature and in the world itself, even in the most banal and trivial of circumstances. We may find rivals coming to the point of murder, obsessed with each other over envious desires for the same object. We may covet lesser objects, such as a piercing or pair of shoes, so long as we have seen them through other people's eyes. Whatever the object the model mediates for the subject, the mechanism is the same. And when internal mediation reaches its height with intense doubling, a tangible object may drop away as the rivals simply become consumed with obsession on each other.

Whether in the social or political realm, internal mediation leads directly to competition, envy, and rivalry through metaphysical desire. Subjects draw dangerously close to their model. They shout: "I want to become like you. I will copy you. I will replace you." This forces the model into a posture of self-defense: either prohibit the imitation or allow it. In either case, we have in internal mediation an endless succession of imitative gestures, escalating the mimetic crisis. The crisis makes doubles out of the subject and model and they become mirrors of one another, scarcely differentiated. The crisis can end only if one or the other person yields. We'll explore in the next chapter what happens when the mimetic crisis reaches its climax.

FOR REFLECTION

Before we move on, let's apply what we've learned in this chapter.

- Are you the kind of person who sometimes wants to trade places with somebody else? If so, why?
- Can you recall a time in your life when you were imitating, whether consciously or unconsciously, the attitudes, behaviors, and goals of another person very close to you? Did you feel like you were being yourself? How did the other person react to you? Did they applaud you or mock you? How did that make you feel and react?
- Let's switch directions. Can you recall a time in your life when another person very close to you copied your words and deeds and made your goals their own? How did that make you feel? How did it affect your relationship with that other person?
- What do you do when someone close to you, a person you admire even, has something you want—love, good health, beauty, success, wealth, wisdom—that they can't share with you? Do you walk away from them? Do you engage in competition with them?
- Have you ever been a double of someone else? How about when someone else has been your double? What was the result? How long did it last and how was it resolved, peacefully or violently and with a sacrifice of some kind?

3

Metaphysical Desire, Contagion, and the Mimetic Crisis

To recap: works of literature like *Beyond the Horizon, A Midsummer Night's Dream,* and some of the other examples we have examined illustrate the dynamics of double mediation and the formation of doubles in the characters' pursuit of concrete desires.

Other works of literature demonstrate metaphysical desire within the characters. Metaphysical desire refers to the intangible desires of one's being. (The prefix *meta* comes from the Latin root for "beyond" or "above" the concrete.) Metaphysical desire can include desire for success, fame, lifestyle, prestige, and so forth. It is "directed beyond objects at some less specific, quasi-transcendent state of well-being or fulfillment."[1] These are existential and abstract desires, a desire for the *being of the other*. Examples of these can be seen in Austin and Lee's role reversals in *True West,* or in Salieri's jealousy of Mozart in *Amadeus*. One person seeks to appropriate another's persona in a futile attempt to grasp at an elusive "something" the other seems to have.

Compared to a concrete desire—for a certain car, fashion, or job, all of which are culturally determined and literally within one's grasp—metaphysical desire can be seen as universal and not physical. Girard believes it exists in all cultures and individuals. After acquiring their basic objects of

1. Kirwan, *Discovering Girard*, 14.

desire, subjects seek to affirm and complete their sheer existence or *being*. Here he explains:

> Once his basic needs are satisfied (indeed, sometimes even before), man is subject to intense desires, though he may not know precisely for what. The reason is that he desires *being* something he himself lacks and which another person seems to possess. The subject thus looks to that other person to inform him of what he should desire in order to acquire that being. If the model, who is already endowed with superior being, desires some object, it must surely be capable of conferring an even greater plentitude of being. It is not through words, therefore, but by the example of his own desire that the model conveys to the subject the supreme desirability of the object.[2]

THE ABSURDITY OF THE SIMPSONS

Metaphysical desire can be seen in popular culture as well as classical works. For over 30 years, the cartoon series *The Simpsons* has satirized the middle class in America. The main characters—parents Homer and Marge, children Bart, Lisa, and Maggie—are known all over the world. In one episode, Bart makes a short film titled "Angry Dad," a cartoon character based on Homer, who has a short temper.[3] It becomes a local success, leading a Hollywood producer to pick it up for mass distribution. Arriving at Bart's house, the producer explains to Bart and Homer how and why Hollywood would remake and distribute the film. Agreeing to the producer's terms, Bart embarks on his adventure; the producer accompanies Bart to Hollywood studios while Homer follows them closely. We don't know as yet why Homer has followed Bart to the studio.

Upon completion of the remake, Bart is invited to a test screening of his movie. It ends up being unanimously rejected by the booing audience. Devastated by the verdict, Bart gives up on his film, but Lisa, his sister, steps in and suggests that if he were to edit all the weak parts out, the movie would make Best Animated Short. After it's edited into a short, Bart's movie wins numerous awards. However, at each awards ceremony, Homer, ever acting like a stumbling block, pushes Bart aside and grabs the prize instead.

---

2. Girard, *Violence and the Sacred*, 146.
3. Nastuk, "Angry Dad."

Metaphysical Desire, Contagion, and the Mimetic Crisis

Early one morning, a Hollywood producer calls Bart with the news that he has won the highest honor, the Academy Award. Homer walks into Bart's bedroom in his bathrobe, both pockets filled with Bart's rightful awards. He asks Bart, "Who called on the telephone?" Bart replies in defense: "Wrong number." He schemes to rid himself of Homer and collect the Academy Award for himself. At that point, when Homer has no chance to claim the coveted award, he congratulates Bart. The rivalry is over.

In its comical way, *The Simpsons* pokes fun at our craving for fame. It's obvious at that moment, when Homer enters Bart's room at five in the morning with awards stuffed in his pockets, that Homer is really collecting glory, not literal prizes. The chase for Bart's Academy Award is a metaphysical surrogate for the recognition Homer desires. He wants the limelight Bart has.

LONGING FOR LIFE IN FILMS

The Akira Kurosawa film *Ikiru* portrays a more subtle metaphysical desire for life and living itself. Kanji Watanabe, a government employee who works incessantly at his desk without ever looking up at his coworkers or life in general, is serious, dry, and wrapped up in his work—so much that one of his staff members, a young girl, Toyo, refers to him as the "mummy." Buried in his paperwork, Watanabe one day learns he has cancer and has only six months left to live. With this news, Watanabe falls into despair and hopelessness. What will he do now? How is he going to confront dying? With minutes and seconds passing by, Watanabe decides not to return to the office that day. Instead, he strolls the streets of Tokyo.

While walking the streets, he meets a writer who proceeds to "teach him how to live." The writer shows him the different sights of the city. Now eager to live his life, Watanabe returns to his house to find yet another unexpected visitor: Toyo. Wishing to resign from the office, she hands her resignation papers to Watanabe to sign. Watanabe signs the forms and accompanies her to the door. On the way, he notices Toyo's stockings are torn; he buys her new stockings and a dinner. Watanabe's generosity leads to a strong friendship between the two until Toyo finds a new job. Watanabe continues to invite her out to dinners and the movies. Uncomfortable at Watanabe's "generosity" and behavior, Toyo finally asks Watanabe why he is behaving so generously. Watanabe explains about his diagnosed cancer and reveals his metaphysical desire to live "life" through Toyo's:

> You are so full of life and . . . and I am envious of that. If I could be like you for one day before I die. I won't be able to die unless I can be . . . .Show me how to be like you.[4]

Kurosawa's *Ikiru* paints the picture of an individual yearning for "life" through another's experience of real life, if only for one day before he dies. This is a picture of metaphysical desire. Many of us may have experienced such longings, especially as teenagers or at a time of life crisis.

A sublime cinematic example of metaphysical desire also appears in the Wim Wenders/Peter Handke film *Der Himmel über Berlin* (*Wings of Desire*). The opening sequence depicts the angels Cassiel and Damiel hovering above the Berlin skies, searching for people in distress so as to comfort them. At the end of each day, they share their thoughts about what they saw and did. By their similar names and by their identical clothing we intuit that Cassiel and Damiel are angels at peace, although they, too, are doubles.

This pacific dynamic changes radically when, after years of watching humans live their lives, Damiel falls in love with a young trapeze artist in a circus. After this, he wishes to become a human being. An encounter with the actor Peter Falk (who becomes the model, playing himself) fuels his desire. Damiel sees Falk one morning at a coffee stand. Having been an angel himself at one time, Falk feels Damiel's presence: "I can't see you, but I know you are there! I feel it. I wish I could see your face, just look into your eyes and tell you how good it is to be here. Just to touch something!"[5] He tells Damiel of the simple joys of life's earthly pleasures:

> Here, to smoke, have coffee. And if you do it together it's fantastic. Or to draw: you know, you take a pencil and you make a dark line, then you make a light line and together it's a good line. Or when your hands are cold, you rub them together, you see, that's good, that feels good! There's so many good things! But you're not here—I'm here. I wish you were here. I wish you could talk to me. 'Cause I'm a friend.[6]

The film suggests that the force of metaphysical desire is so strong, even angels can fall to it: they can want to be fully human, to see colors, to have blood, taste a hot cup of coffee, have friendships, and be in love. Letting such metaphysical desires take over, Damiel follows Falk's example and

---

4. Kurosawa, *Seven Samurai and Other Screenplays*, 32.
5. Wenders and Hanke, *Der Himmel über Berlin*, translated as *Wings of Desire*, 122.
6. Wenders and Hanke, *Der Himmel über Berlin*, 123.

"takes the jump." Becoming a human, Damiel proceeds to find the trapeze artist with whom he has fallen in love.

In these literary and cinematic examples, we have seen doubles generate vicious envy and rivalry as a product of internal mediation and intersecting spheres of desire. We have also seen that, after subjects have satisfied their basic material needs, they project their needs into the metaphysical realm. Film especially suggests metaphysical desires to their suggestable audiences, as you may have seen or experienced yourself.

Conversely, the upending of our personal lives can trigger a crisis of metaphysical desire. In *True West* and *A Midsummer Night's Dream*, double mediation causes the protagonists to lose their identity. They search for their own character, their own personality, and their own lives, as seen in another person's life. Lee desires the life of Austin; Austin desires to become, or to *be*, Lee. Matters are even more complicated among the doubling couples of *A Midsummer Night's Dream*.

TWO TRAMPS AND ETERNITY: A PARALYSIS OF DOUBLES

What becomes of metaphysical desire in the end? The horror of doubles and thwarted metaphysical desire can spread to the entire world and become an emblem of the human condition. Let us look at Samuel Beckett's play *Waiting for Godot*. The curtain rises on one of the most famous doubles in modern literature: two tramps, Vladimir and Estragon, are standing in an empty landscape. They are dressed alike; their language is bare and minimal. The audiences who first saw this play, written in French in 1948–1949, after the devastation of World War II, would have understood the context of this emptiness. The play provokes the war-weary audience with the question: What happens after a holocaust?

The tramps are in a crisis. They are waiting for a certain Mr. Godot to arrive, but he does not appear. The plot reveals that the tramps have no option but to wait and keep on waiting. They want to leave, and repeatedly they declare they will go. But they realize that they can't, for they have to wait for Godot's arrival. Unable to move, the tramps remain on the very same spot throughout the entire play. They even contemplate "repenting," but that does not go very far. There's no one to blame, no one they can fault for being in this crisis. Realizing this, they place the blame on their very existence:

Vladimir: Gogo.

> Estragon: What?
>
> Vladimir: Suppose we repented.
>
> Estragon: Repented what?
>
> Vladimir: Oh . . . (*He reflects.*) We wouldn't have to go into details.
>
> Estragon: Our being born?[7]

They finally decide to kill themselves. Unable to decide who should kill himself first, they do not, and cannot carry out the deed. They remain frozen in paralysis. Trapped in an undifferentiated reality of time and space, they do the only thing they can: wait.

Into this landscape two more characters appear: Lucky and Pozzo, a master and his slave. Pozzo, with a whip in his hands, dominates Lucky, who Pozzo leads like an animal with a rope around his neck. Lucky obeys Pozzo, never letting go of the heavy burden. We don't know where they are coming from, who they are, or why they are in their current position.

Estragon takes pity on Lucky, who begins crying, offering him a handkerchief Pozzo gives him, only to get kicked by Lucky in the shins. Estragon retaliates by spitting in Lucky's face. The farce continues as Pozzo commands Lucky, at the tramps' request, to dance and think, which he does, going on an absurdist philosophical rant.

A messenger-boy appears at the end of the first act. The tramps ask the boy numerous questions before getting to Godot. Coming to the point, the boy finally delivers his message: "Mr. Godot told me to tell you he won't come this evening but surely to-morrow."[8] Once again, the tramps contemplate leaving:

> Estragon: Well, shall we go?
>
> Vladimir: Yes, let's go.
>
> *They do not move.*[9]

And the curtain falls. The second act ("Next day. Same time. Same place."), like the first, consists of pauses, silences, and futility. Vladimir cries out: "Say something!"[10] Estragon: "I'm trying."[11] The very ability to communicate

---

7. Beckett, *Waiting for Godot*, 373.
8. Beckett, *Waiting for Godot*, 423.
9. Beckett, *Waiting for Godot*, 427.
10. Beckett, *Waiting for Godot*, 436.
11. Beckett, *Waiting for Godot*, 437.

Metaphysical Desire, Contagion, and the Mimetic Crisis

falters. Words fail in this crisis of metaphysical desire. All Vladimir and Estragon can do is wait for Godot, who never comes. Actions fail, too, as the tramps prove incapable of helping Pozzo, who returns to the scene blind and no longer able to dominate Lucky. Vladimir meets Pozzo's cries for pity with a blow. The two finally try to help Pozzo, but they fail. In this tragicomic environment, the play seems to be saying, humankind is capable of violent acts only, or else it is incapable of acting at all. Receiving neither help nor pity from the tramps, Pozzo and Lucky exit the stage. The messenger boy returns with the news that Godot would not be coming today, but that he will be doing so tomorrow without fail. Thus the play concludes, establishing a circular view of time and history as the tramps repeat themselves:

> Vladimir: Well? Shall we go?
>
> Estragon: Yes, let's go.
>
> *They do not move.*
> Curtain[12]

Like Austin and Lee of *True West*, Vladimir and Estragon present us with doubles who have become fixated on one another; indeed, from our first encounter of them we find that they share one persona, and they have no ability, no reason, and no space by which they can separate from one another. In its minimalism, *Waiting for Godot* portrays the phenomenon of doubles with a stark philosophical accent. The play distills human violence to its essence and offers no solution for it. Vladimir's and Estragon's identities mirror one another to the point of infinity. Even their shabby clothing and nonsensical nicknames, Didi and Gogo, reveal their similarity. From such uniformity and paralysis there seems to be no return, no way back. Indeed, as with *True West*, *Waiting for Godot* ends without resolution for its hapless doubles: the cycle repeats itself. The play exemplifies post-World War II and holocaust pessimism and despair.

Waiting for Godot embodies Beckett's harrowing and personal response to the ghastly wars of the twentieth century. Beckett labeled his play a "tragicomedy": he tries to articulate the *tragedy* of human existence, but it is also a *comedy* because the human condition after World War II is absurd and can only be portrayed as such. Dramatically speaking, waiting for Godot to arrive proves an impossible task. Our metaphysical desire for *life* is unattainable. The cataclysm of World War II has occurred, an event inconceivable by human imagination, logic, or reason. Yet it happened. It

---

12. Beckett, *Waiting for Godot*, 476.

was, as with most wars—inconceivable, horrific, and inexcusable. The paralysis of doubles spreads to the entire community—in this case, it becomes the human condition itself. Beckett's portrayal of the tramp doubles acts like a philosophical treatise against humankind. They embody a human race capable of unspeakable wars waged without reason, recourse, or redemption. They also embody humanity's powerlessness—with its inability to take action against the sacrificial brutality of concentration camps, with its barbed wires and burnt skin, charred flesh, and bones.

CONTAGION

The formation of doubles signals an alarm. What brothers or sisters want to be the same as their siblings? Who wants to see a duplicate walking, talking, and dressing just like them? By all measures, most individuals do their best *not* to resemble their siblings or others in society. But when doubles form, it can become impossible to stop their multiplication. Much like a domino effect in which the first to fall triggers the rest, one set of doubles gives rise to the next. As we saw in *A Midsummer Night's Dream*, the process can continue until the entire community mirrors the same identity and desires. The lack of division between people caused by mimetic contagion signals the presence of a building mimetic crisis within the community: a desire no longer belongs to just *one* or *two* individuals; it belongs to *all* individuals in the community desiring the *same object*.

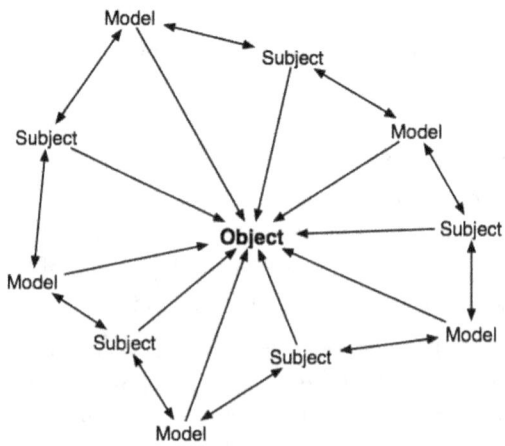

Figure 3: Contagion

Metaphysical Desire, Contagion, and the Mimetic Crisis

The spread throughout the community becomes total. As contagion spreads, the mimetic crisis heightens. Its escalation across society often leads to violence.

Let's look at a benign, humorous example satirizing this dynamic from pop culture. In an episode of the TV comedy *Seinfeld*, "The Bookstore,"[13] Jerry Seinfeld's family and friends become ensnared in a wave of shoplifting. The plot begins at Tom's Restaurant, where we find Seinfeld confronting Uncle Leo for stealing a book from Brentano's. His uncle refuses to take responsibility:

> JERRY: Leo, I saw you steal.
>
> LEO: Oh, they don't care. We all do it.
>
> JERRY: Who, criminals?
>
> LEO: Senior citizens. No big deal.
>
> JERRY: You could get arrested.
>
> LEO: Arrested? Come on! I'm an old man. I'm confused! I thought I paid for it. What's my name? Will you take me home?

Jerry takes it upon himself to ensure justice by asking the security guards to scare his uncle away from Brentano's. The guard obliges Jerry's demand immediately:

> JERRY: (To himself) I don't believe this! (Walks over to a security guard) Excuse me, I wonder if you could do me a favor? My uncle's having a little problem with shoplifting.
>
> GUARD: Mm-hmm. Where's your uncle?
>
> JERRY: (Pointing) He's over there in the overcoat. If you could just kind of put a scare into him. You know, set him straight..
>
> GUARD: (Into his walkie-talkie) We have a 51–50 in paperbacks. All units respond.
>
> JERRY: "51–50"? That—that's just a scare, right?
>
> GUARD: Sir, I'm gonna have to ask you to stand out of the way and let us handle this. (The guard rushes toward Uncle Leo.) Swarm! Swarm!
>
> (Suddenly, Leo is surrounded by guards.)
>
> LEO: What? I'm an old man! I'm confused!
>
> GUARD: You're under arrest.

13. Ackerman, "Bookstore."

Later, at Jerry's apartment, we find him talking to his parents on the telephone about Uncle Leo. In defense of Uncle Leo, Jerry's parents admit to their share of shoplifting, their justification being, "Nobody pays for everything" and "It's not stealing if it's something you need." Jerry asks them what his parents were stealing and why. What was it that was so worth stealing?

> MORTY: Nothing. Batteries. (Jerry scoffs.) Well, they wear out so quick.
>
> JERRY: Mom, you too?
>
> HELEN: Sometimes your father forgets, so I have to steal them.

Jerry begins to regret reporting Uncle Leo to the security guards. To amend the mistake, he walks back to Brentano's to speak to the manager about the incident. While he is waiting for the manager, Jerry's friend George greets him—and heads off to steal a book! Now the manager arrives:

> MANAGER: Did you want to speak with the manager?
>
> JERRY: Yes. My Uncle Leo was caught shoplifting here the other day.
>
> MANAGER: Yes, Uncle Leo. I remember him. I'm sorry, our policy is we prosecute all shoplifters.

Pleading to the manager, Jerry makes a familiar-sounding appeal: "Oh, come on. He's just a lonely old man. All old people steal." At this point that the manager pronounces a solution:

> MANAGER: That's right. That's why we stopped carrying batteries. Look, I'll be honest with you, we've had a lot of trouble with theft lately—and my boss says I have to make an example of someone.

Jerry thinks quickly: catching just *one* shoplifter will solve the problem.

> JERRY: So it could be anyone?
>
> MANAGER: I guess. As long as we catch him in the act.
>
> (Jerry turns to George. George has a huge bundle under his overcoat and is trying to act innocent.)
>
> JERRY: That guy! (Pointing at George.) Swarm! Swarm!
>
> (George is instantly surrounded by guards)
>
> GEORGE: No! Jerry!

Metaphysical Desire, Contagion, and the Mimetic Crisis

This comic plot may seem absurd, but it reveals a truth about desire. We don't even need to see the object the model makes desirable in order for us to want it. Rather, mere hearsay will do. The characters in *Seinfeld* stoke the forbidden desire to shoplift through gossip, innuendo, and rumors. These are enough to make the taboo attractive. Mere talk about an object of desire casts a spotlight it, enticing others to talk about it. Contagion spreads from one person to another until it has an entire community "infected." The course of mimetic contagion is unpredictable. It's difficult to mark its beginning or to chart its direction, because contagion behaves like a plague.

The real-life case of the 1938 radio broadcast of *The War of the Worlds* in New York City illustrates the potential for a mimetic crisis to multiply rapidly. Originally intended as a theatrical hoax at Halloween by producer and narrator Orson Welles, the evening broadcast used music and fake news bulletins to pretend an alien invasion had landed in New Jersey and overwhelmed the United States. Although the extent of actual panic that night seemed limited (phone calls to local police stations increased by 40% that night), the news media jumped on the story and created the urban myth that there had been widespread panic. The papers claimed that men, women, and children had choked the streets fleeing in terror or attempted suicide out of fear of an alien invasion in "a collective, nationwide schizophrenia":

> An unidentified announcer broke in during the [regular] broadcast with prime news of the landing of the Martians in New Jersey; then from time to time, [there were] other communications of this sort, including a dramatic speech from the Secretary of the Interior; finally the President came on to confirm the gravity of the situation. [. . .] This was all it took for thousands of thousands and finally millions of listeners to believe that the end of the world had come. The consequences of this panic were celebrated: people fled in all directions, those from the city to the country and vice versa. In the dead of night, highways were streaked with innumerable cars. Priests were called to hear confessions. There were miscarriages, broken limbs, in the scuffles, heart attacks; hospitals and psychiatric centers didn't know how to cope with the rush of patients.[14]

The newspapers created a contagious scare story about what had happened that persists to this day. Rumors both create and illustrate mimetic

---

14. Bazin, *Orson Welles*, 47–48.

contagion. Taking shape through fads, fashion, or herd mentality, mimetic contagion can be small or large, comic or tragic. It can also easily be fostered through the feeding of metaphysical desire. Remember how Don Quixote's zeal to be like the "greatest" and "most noble" knight, Amadis of Gaul, communicated itself to everyone around him in Cervantes's novel? People were swept up in hysteria in a fictional world suggested originally by one person, but which spread to the entire community.

Once contagion starts, it becomes almost impossible to stop, and no one knows how quickly and where it will spread next. René Girard underscores the metaphor of contamination: "Metaphysical desire is always contagious. The metaphysical desire becomes even more so as the mediator draws nearer to the hero. Contagion and proximity are, after all, one and the same phenomenon. Internal mediation is present when one 'catches' a nearby desire just as one would catch the plague or cholera, simply by contact with an infected person."[15] Contagion can easily multiply and spread from two people to others via doubles until it "infects" countless numbers of people and the entire society is exposed. As with all plagues, it can happen quickly and destructively. The danger of mimetic contagion lies in its contamination of the community with negative and destructive models.

FOR REFLECTION

Before we move on, let's apply what we've learned in this chapter.

- What are your most deeply held values? What traits do you admire the most? How did these become your most cherished values and traits? Who or what made these attractive to you?
- Would you say that you have been successful at realizing your most highly valued character traits and virtues? If so, how, and if not, why not?
- Have you had the experience of being caught up in the latest fad in clothing, food, lifestyle, music, sports, etc.? What was that experience like for you? Did the fad become a habit or did you eventually lose interest?
- Contagion can take positive, constructive forms (such as the Ice Bucket Challenge to raise money for research to cure ALS) and negative,

---

15. Girard, *Deceit, Desire, and the Novel: Self and Other in Literary Structure*, 99.

destructive forms (like political conspiracy theories like QAnon). Have you either knowingly or unknowingly been part of a "craze," whether cultural, social, or political? Have you ever helped spread a rumor?

4

The Sacrificial Crisis and the Scapegoat Mechanism

WIDESPREAD CONTAGION

DURING THE DEVASTATING CORONAVIRUS pandemic, incidents of violent racial crimes against Asian-Americans rose significantly across the United States. In addition, George Floyd, a Black man, was murdered at the hands of a Minneapolis police officer. It may not have occurred to you that the scourge of COVID-19 and the scourge of racism relate to each other. But they do. Both are examples of social contagion. As we've seen from examples from *Seinfeld, A Clockwork Orange*, anorexia, the craze for piercing, or rumors spread by neighbors or newspapers, contagion can work on any level and scale—visible or invisible, inviting or threatening. Although contagions can sometimes be positive, René Girard's work is especially concerned with what happens when things go bad. In the final analysis negative contagion works to create proximity and sameness between individuals through mimetic desire, rendering an entire population without difference. This can happen between individuals, within a particular community, or throughout a whole society.

Girard illuminates this process and its connection to internal mediation when he writes, "In the world of internal mediation, the contagion is

The Sacrificial Crisis and the Scapegoat Mechanism

so widespread that everyone can become his neighbor's mediator [model] without ever understanding the role he is playing."[1] Inevitably, in each social circle where people share the same values, ideas, or goals, contagion will spread, influencing the social structures. In the contagion-struck society, what appears to be the widespread "norm" may simply be reflecting subjects who have been unknowingly and mimetically mediated and who have fallen into the trap of desire. Slight differences between people will always be present, of course, but they are small enough so as to remain insignificant compared to the largely undifferentiated crowd. Girard shows how widespread contagion can lead to what he calls the **crisis of undifferentiation** or the **sacrificial crisis**.

In such mimetic crises, communities cannot understand the cause or correctly assign blame for the contagion. As the crisis and confusion comes to a head, Girard shows us how as the crowd searches fruitlessly for a cause, they may suddenly point an accusatory finger at a random person or group of people, holding them responsible for the crisis. Then comes a shocking resolution: upon falling upon their innocent (yet perceived as guilty) victim, the community members first unanimously accuse this individual (or group of individuals) of crimes, and then "sacrifice" them so that peace and order will be restored. Haven't we all seen something like this happen, from office politics to national politics? There's even a name for such a person taking the blame for others: "fall guy." When things at the office get tense, a certain person—an innocent person—may get fired. Someone in the entertainment industry may be blackballed and kept from getting work. When politicians lie or engage in illegal behavior, instead of everyone being held accountable, one unlucky soul may end up going to jail. Sometimes the person even accepts taking the hit for the community as a whole! Maybe you've been part of such a scenario or even been the victim. After the crisis in which the inability to distinguish doubles and locate the source of the "plague" comes to a head, the community converges on and sacrifices a **scapegoat** to restore order and peace in the community. With the literal or figurative death of an innocent victim, the crisis of undifferentiation, or what we will refer to as the sacrificial crisis, resolves. Here we have the second of Girard's great insights.

In discussing the metaphor of the plague for mimetic contagion—in everyday life as well as in world literature and mythology—Girard makes the following observations:

---

1. Girard, *Deceit, Desire, and the Novel*, 99.

> The theme spans the whole range of literary and even non-literary genres, from pure fantasy to the most positive and scientific accounts. It is older than literature—much older, really, since it is present in myth and ritual in the entire world. . . . The plague is universally presented as a process of undifferentiation, a destruction of specificities. This destruction is often proceeded by a reversal. The plague will turn the honest man into a thief, the virtuous man into a lecher, the prostitute into a saint. Friends murder and enemies embrace. Political and religious authorities collapse. The plague makes all accumulated knowledge and all categories of judgment invalid.[2]

The "reversal" caused by the plague erases differences between individuals and their social roles. In the place of one's original status and identity, the crisis or "plague" replaces them with their opposites, undoing society's structure and meaning. A panic ensues—someone must be responsible for the plague. At the height of this breakdown of difference and meaning, the frenzied crowd converges on and sacrifices a random person or group, turning against them in a unanimous, all-against-one motion—the whole community against the victim. In the eyes of the plague-ridden community, the victim's sacrifice must be required to restore normalcy, peace, and order to the society. Girard expands on the arbitrary nature of scapegoating:

> The process [of scapegoating] just described implies that the random victim must be perceived as a "real culprit," missing before and now identified and punished. The random victim, in other words, will never be perceived as random; the "cure" would not be operative if its benefactors realized the randomness of the victim's selection. . . . If the collective transfer is really effective, the victim will never appear as an explicit scapegoat, as an innocent destroyed by the blind passion of the crowd. This victim will pass for a real criminal, for the one guilty exception in a community now emptied of its violence.[3]

Although all this may sound abstract, it's easy to find many concrete examples in contemporary social and political events, culture, literature, and mythology. Perhaps the narrative that most clearly and powerfully illustrates what Girard calls the scapegoat mechanism is the short story "The Lottery," written in 1948 by Shirley Jackson. It's a bald and straightforward representation of a scapegoating scene. In this story, the whole community

---

2. Girard, *To Double Business Bound*, 136–37.
3. Girard, *To Double Business Bound*, 146.

The Sacrificial Crisis and the Scapegoat Mechanism

of a small, ordinary town gathers once a year in June for an annual ritual called the lottery. This scene of ordinary Americana soon turns sinister, however. Families stand together; the young and old, men and women, all reverently desiring to participate, as if there were a great reward to be won. Each person in the town takes turns drawing a piece of paper from a black wooden box. When all have equally taken their turn, we see a moment of undifferentiation. But then, one person gets the paper marked with an "X," differentiating them. The "winner," holding the marked piece of paper, is then collectively stoned to death by the other members of the community—friends and family members alike. The story has horrified readers for generations and generated a record amount of mail when it was published.

"The Lottery" vividly demonstrates at once both mimetic desire and the sacrificial crisis at work. First, the citizens of the town *unanimously* play the lottery, and their desire to survive becomes a contagion; second, the game leads to *undifferentiation*, as each person playing the lottery takes a piece of paper and becomes an equal of everyone else—until the moment when the crowd identifies and sacrifices the victim-scapegoat; third, the game, by its very nature, shows the *arbitrary* nature of the scapegoat and the sacrifice involved to resolve the sacrificial crisis; and fourth, the lottery repeats annually, thereby establishing it as a *ritual*.

Another well-known depiction of the scapegoating process in literature comes from William Golding's novel, *Lord of the Flies* (1954). A group of young boys find themselves stranded on an island after their airplane has crashed. Without any structure, law, or supervision, the group of castaways has no identity. Gradually, the boys on the island form groups, establish teams, and choose leaders from the different groups. This establishment of law and order, however, comes at the price of violence and a sacrifice. One youngster, Piggy, who the other boys constantly pick on for being overweight and wearing eyeglasses, is finally chased down by the rest and killed. The murder of Piggy temporarily resolves the crisis, but the collective descends into tribal savagery. The orgy of violence ends only when a naval ship arrives in rescue.

The scapegoat mechanism, even in this bald form, unfortunately has not ended to this day—and it's not just found in fiction. It still can be found in different communities around the world. Anywhere we have money, politics, and power at work, we have the potential of having the scapegoat mechanism. Written and directed in 2017 by the Zambian-British filmmaker Rungano Nyoni and winner of Cannes Festival's Camera d'Or prize, the film *I Am Not a Witch* illustrates the haunting nature of the scapegoat mechanism and how the innocent become its victims, by depicting how real witch camps in Zambia function in that society.

The film opens with a busload of tourists pulling up to see and photograph a witch camp. Having bought their expensive tickets, they proceed to look at the witches. Behind a metal barricade and attached to white ribbons sit about twenty middle age and elder women with white make up on their faces, on the ground with their legs stretched out, staring out at the tourists. The ribbons roll together around a spool. One tourist asks the guide, "What the ribbons are for?" The guide responds, "They are to prevent the witches from flying," adding "The witches can fly as far as UK." Highlighting their dangerous nature, the guide adds these witches have the power of flying and killing people. Captured and imprisoned at the witch camp, attached to the ribbons, the witches are now considered harmless and put on display for people and tourists. Thrilled and amazed, the tourists take pictures and ask more questions to satisfy their curiosity. To make their display realistic and terrifying, the witches break out to sing a song, waving their hands and making faces.

Who are these witches? Where do they come from? Are they real witches with supernatural powers? All these questions arise. As contemporary audiences we may believe witches don't exist and they aren't real. And how come there are no men?

The answer to our questions begins to unfold in the next scene. A middle-aged woman draws water from a well. As she fills her bucket with water, places it on her head, and takes a few steps, she stumbles and falls. The camera cuts to a young girl, just eight or nine years old, standing on the path and looking at the woman on the ground. The woman looks at girl and then runs away. Then in the next scene we see the young girl placing the bucket, now filled with water, on the stairs of the woman's house. She knocks at the door and gets no answer, so she places the bucket on the stairs and sits down beside it. Looking through the window, the middle-aged woman ignores the girl, though it appears she is only trying to help. But the woman misinterprets her good-will act of charity.

In the scene that follows, we find the woman and the girl at the police station, where the woman accuses the girl of being a witch. The woman tells the police officer the girl has no name or friends and that a lot of strange things have been happening ever since she entered the village—now the well is poisonous, and no one dares use the water. A mob of villagers joins

The Sacrificial Crisis and the Scapegoat Mechanism

in the accusations in excitement. At one point, a farmer crawls into the office through the window to give testimony against the young girl, claiming the girl must indeed be a witch, because she had attacked him with an ax and cut off his arm. The officer asks what he did next, to which the farmer responds he realized it was a bad dream, but as a result the dream his wife has been going to the farm instead of him!

The nameless young girl remains silent throughout the investigation and accusations. She neither affirms nor denies being a witch. Unsure how to proceed with the girl, the officer calls her superior, Mr. Banda, to ask what she should do. He tells the officer not to do anything, but to be careful, as witches can be very deceptive, conniving, and dangerous. Mr. Banda brings in a witch doctor, and using a chicken, a song and a dance, the witch doctor determines the young girl is indeed a witch. Having the certification of the witch doctor, Mr. Banda takes the girl to the witch camp and introduces her to the local queen and heads of government, who attentively listen to him give his presentation.

Standing under a blanket, the young girl is unveiled. She tries to run away but doesn't get far as Mr. Banda orders his men to catch her. Caught and shamed for trying to run away from the camp, they attach a ribbon to her back and force her to join the witches. The witches initiate her to how to be a witch, teaching how the witches and civil servants work together on behalf of the government—they are "civil" witches.

At night, the fire in the camp lights the next scene. To the rhythm of the drums and music, the witches salute Mr. Banda, dance and sing the upbeat national song. The refrain cries, "We are soldiers for the government, and we are used to it. / We are used to it, and we don't get tired." With a ribbon attached to her back, the girl is brought to a wooden hut to stay overnight. She has one night to think about her choice: if she cuts the ribbon she will become a chicken, but if she keeps the ribbon, she can join the witch camp.

The next morning, Mr. Banda—with his men and the witches behind him—knocks on the door and asks: "Is there a witch inside?" The young girl walks out. After everyone applauds and rejoices at the girl's decision, the witches, along with the girl, go to a farm in an orange government truck to do manual labor. The truck not only carries the women-witches, but it also carries their spool of white ribbon hanging from metal poles. A grandmother figures gives the young girl the name Shula—meaning the uprooted one.

By now, it's become clear for the audience that though a local queen is supposedly in charge, the local village and area is a patriarchal society run by men—with Mr. Banda overseeing everything. Shortly after Shula becomes a full pledged witch, Mr. Banda takes her under his wing and they go on a TV show to show her off, where he calls her "my little witch." He asks Shula to do impossible tasks with her witch power. Unhappy with the works of the witches, the queen demands to see Mr. Banda. Furious, the queen complains about the terrible drought that has plagued her kingdom. She wants to know why the witches don't bring rain, as Mr. Banda promised they would.

The community pressures Shula to bring down rain; if she is a witch, she should be able to bring down rain. She dances but nothing happens. Fed up with her status and life as a witch, at nighttime before sleeping she tells the other witches she should have chosen to be a goat, because as a goat she would have been free to go anywhere. Her fellow witches respond by telling her that they would have killed her and eaten her. While the witches sleep, she leaves the room, goes outside and cuts her ribbon.

The next scene shows two locals carrying her wrapped in white sheets to the field in their cart. They place her on the ground and leave. Shortly after, the first witch runs to Shula's corpse and begins to cry and the other witches join them. They sing a song to celebrate her life: "Come, let us sing for Shula, this celebration is the final one / This celebration is for mourning / this celebration, my friends is for Shula, is the final one." The song ends and now we find the witches sitting around in a circle. A heavy rain begins to pour down on the witches and the ground. Was the death of Shula necessary for the rain? The final scene shows the orange truck with the spools of white ribbon. The ribbons have been cut and waver in the air. The wavering ribbons act as a metaphor for political and emotional freedom.

Written as a criticism of Zambian government and politics, Nyoni's *I Am Not a Witch* brilliantly shows that all it takes is a simple small lie and accusation—a random irrational spark—to start off the scapegoat mechanism. The little girl Shula serves as a perfect target to become a scapegoat: she was without name, without a family or friends, and simply arrived with goodwill, saw a woman carrying a bucket of water stumble and fall, and tried to help. Like many before her, she was accused of being a witch.

While witch figures have existed ever since ancient times in folklore, stories, myths and literature, artists didn't use them to show the scapegoat mechanism until the twentieth century. We find the witch figure Hecate as early as in the ancient Greek myth of "Demeter and Persephone" (6 BCE) and again in Ovid's Roman epic poem *Metamorphoses* (8 AD). Later, we find the three witches in Shakespeare's tragedy *Macbeth* as well. But twentieth-century literature, drama and film narratives took a radical turn in their use of witch figures. Rather than simply using them as literary figures as in Shakespeare's play, modern artists began depicting witches as victims of the scapegoat mechanism. Arthur Miller's *The Crucible*, written midcentury in 1953, best depicts the scapegoat mechanism using witch figures. A historical drama based on the 1692–1693 Salem witch trials, it also acts as an allegory about 1950s McCarthyism in which various actors, writers, directors and government officials were accused of being communists.[4] Like the story in "The Lottery," we see how the whole community converges on a random person or group in a contagious, mimetic frenzy.

The sacrificial mechanism of scapegoating works within small communities as well as larger ones. We're all familiar with political crises that threaten to destroy the whole nation or even the whole world. What we commonly call "war" we can see as nothing less than a sacrificial crisis between different leaders and nations. A highly oscillated and contagious conflict arises between the two or more belligerent parties over a disputed object of desire, leading to the sacrificial crisis, in which one or more persons or parties needs to be blamed (that is, scapegoated) for the crisis and sacrificed to end the conflict. With the execution or sacrifice of the scapegoat, a temporary peace and order descends on the community, which maintains a fragile equilibrium until the next crisis arises.

The Humphrey Cobb novel *Paths of Glory* made into a film by Stanley Kubrick in 1957, recounts a real-life historical battle between the French and Germans during World War I. It portrays the explicit scapegoating and sacrifice of three soldiers as a result of a failed attack to regain French territory occupied by Germans. Internal conflict embroils the French army: General Broulard (the corps commander of the division) and General Rousseau (the commander of the division) want to attack Anthill and capture it under any circumstances. On the other hand, Colonel Dax (the commander of the regiment) views the scheme as a suicide mission and opposes the plan. Pulling rank, General Rousseau and General Broulard

---

4. Arthur Miller himself was accused and questioned, as were film directors such as Elia Kazan and Charlie Chaplin. In response to the accusation, Chaplin went back to his native country of the United Kingdom and made *A King in New York* (1957) a black comedy and satire based on his experience in US during McCarthyism. He only returned to the United States in 1972 to receive a Life-Time Achievement Academy Award.

order Colonel Dax to lead his soldiers to take over Anthill, even though it's an impossible order to carry out under the torrent of the German attackers' fire. Some soldiers remain in the trench while others move forward, only to face their certain death.

The attempt to recapture Anthill fails miserably. The superiors order Dax and his troops to try a second time, but they fight to no avail. Facing dishonor before the army and his superiors, General Rousseau throws blame for the failed attack onto the soldiers themselves: a soldier will be picked from each division to be court-martialed. Soldiers are randomly selected from each division and charged with mutiny. One soldier gets picked because he's considered socially unpleasant and unacceptable; a second is selected because he knows the truth about his superior's abandonment of his soldiers during the attack; and the third—a stellar soldier with distinction—has his name drawn through a lottery.

With his regiment accused of crimes they didn't commit, Colonel Dax objects to the plan. Rather than participate in the deception, he sides with his soldiers and represents them at the hearing. Well aware of what General Rousseau and General Broulard are doing, he brings up the subject to General Broulard as early on as their initial exchange:

Colonel Dax

And you're certainly not interested in digging up scapegoats for the staff's mistake? . . . Let's lay it on the line. The staff is looking for sacrificial goats, but it's too squeamish—not to mention, cautious—to do its own slaughtering.[5]

General Broulard, taken aback by Colonel Dax's remarks, mockingly dismisses them. According to him, no scapegoats exist. Rather, a few soldiers are simply being justly executed as examples for the rest of the army: he believes these soldiers truly at fault and the generals innocent of any wrongdoing.

General Broulard

Colonel really! That sounds like one of those still-beating-your-wife queries. But, no, certainly not. We are not looking for scapegoats.[6]

---

5. Kubrick and Thompson, *Paths of Glory*, 76.
6. Kubrick and Thompson, *Paths of Glory*, 76.

The Sacrificial Crisis and the Scapegoat Mechanism

In the course of the conversation, General Broulard points out the execution of the soldiers serves to set an example for the rest. Finishing this conversation with Colonel Dax, General Broulard asks him to select the soldiers. But refusing to go along with the scheme, Colonel Dax offers a self-sacrificial solution—the substitution of himself for the prisoner/soldiers:

> Gentlemen, if it's an example you want, one man will do as well as a hundred. But I wouldn't know how to choose him. I will have to offer myself—after all I'm the responsible officer.[7]

An exchange ensues between the officers about the innocence of the soldiers and the arbitrary nature of the scapegoating action. It becomes clear that, more than anyone, these officers have deciphered and understood scapegoating and the mechanism that creates sacrificial victims. One of the officers of the regiment, Captain Sancy, remarks:

> All the men are equally innocent. None of them's showed cowardice, but one of them's got to be shot for it, nonetheless. Now the point is which one?[8]

Lieutenant Jonnart, in charge of selecting one soldier for the court martial, has a solution:

> But orders are orders and one of you has to be chosen. The fairest way is to draw lots. There are one hundred and eleven slips in this box. One slip is marked with a cross. The man who draws it will go before the court martial.[9]

Paths of Glory shows many uncanny similarities to the short story "The Lottery." In both, the court-martialed soldiers and the unlucky villager who "wins" the lottery stand in no direct relation to their undeserved punishment, and the victimizers go to great lengths to conceal this reality. Moreover, neither Jackson's story nor Cobb's novel flinches from this banal but terrible truth: the crowd chooses scapegoats in a thoroughly trivial manner.

While *Paths of Glory* illustrates the role of the scapegoating mechanism, it also reveals that only a single scapegoat is needed to stand in for many. Recall the words of Colonel Dax: "Gentlemen, if it's an example you

---

7. Kubrick and Thompson, *Paths of Glory*, 81.
8. Kubrick and Thompson, *Paths of Glory*, 81.
9. Kubrick and Thompson, *Paths of Glory*, 96.

want, one man will do as well as a hundred." On the other hand, in an atmosphere of accusation, scapegoats can multiply. Once activated, scapegoating can rapidly ramp up with a limitless field of victimage. A local crisis suddenly becomes a global crisis. Think about the causes of the first World War: one day in 1914, Archduke Franz Ferdinand was assassinated; two years later, one million men were killed or wounded in the Battle of the Somme.

Scapegoats multiply easily in times of war and global conflict. If we study modern history, we find the course of the sacrificial crisis oscillating repeatedly into disasters of pandemic proportions. World War I (1914–1918) was mentioned, but that was just the start as we also had the Armenian genocide (1915–1917); the purges under Stalin in the Soviet Union (1920s–1930s); the *Shoah* or Jewish holocaust during World War II (1939–1945); the persecutions and famines that killed tens of millions in the People's Republic of China (1950s–1970s); the "ethnic cleansing" of Bosnia (1990s); the Rwandan genocide (1994); and the Darfur genocide (2003), among other calamities. Scapegoating isn't just a fictional theme—it bedevils our real world everywhere.

THE SCAPEGOAT

Let's delve further into the role and meaning of the scapegoat. The multilayered term "scapegoat" spans all of human history. Girard points out three different meanings: a biblical meaning, an anthropological meaning, and a psychosocial meaning:

1. *The biblical meaning.* In the Mosaic ritual of the Day of Atonement (Lev 16), the scapegoat is "one of the two goats that was chosen by lot to be sent alive into the wilderness, the sins of the people having been symbolically laid upon it, while the other was appointed to be sacrificed."[10] "Scapegoat" is as good a term as any other to designate, in the Leviticus ritual, the first of the two goats and the function it is called on to perform.

2. *The anthropological meaning.* Beginning with the eighteenth century, or before, analogies were perceived between the Leviticus ritual and other rituals. In his book on India, for instance, Raynal observed that "they have a scape-horse, analogous to the scape-goat of the Jews.

10. Burkert et al., *Violent Origins*, 73.

The Sacrificial Crisis and the Scapegoat Mechanism

... " In the nineteenth and twentieth centuries, Frazer and others freely utilized the term scapegoat in connection with a large number of rituals. These rituals, they felt, were based on the belief that "guilt" or "suffering" could be transferred from some community to a ritually designed victim, often an animal but sometimes a human being, the Greek *pharmakos*, for instance. . . . [11]

3. *The psychosocial meaning.* In popular novels, conversations, newspaper articles, and so on, the victim or victims of unjust violence or discrimination are called scapegoats, especially when they are blamed or punished not merely for the "sins" of others, as most dictionaries assert, but for the tensions, conflicts and difficulties of all kinds. In connection with "scapegoat" in this third sense, the English language has forged such words as "scapegoat" and "scapegoating." In the present essay, I will use these words only when these psychosocial connotations are implied.[12]

René Girard studied archaic myths, societies, and civilizations. He discovered the same mechanism consistently at work to resolve and end cycles of violence. He also found a common thread: a community in crisis perceives its unhappy situation to be the responsibility of an arbitrarily selected victim or group of victims, and the community unanimously and arbitrarily sacrifices this scapegoat (or **surrogate victim**) to restore peace and order in the community.

Girard uses Shakespeare's historical play *Julius Caesar* to illustrate the sacrificial mechanism at work in *all* the political parties of Rome. All the senators desire the same object: Caesar's position of absolute power. In his speech to Caius Cassius, Brutus describes the assassination of Caesar as a collective *all-against-one* murder. Note Brutus's consistent plural choice of language: "*Let's* be," "*We all*," "*we* could come," "And gentle *friends*," "*Let's* kill him," "*Let's* carve," "let *our* hearts," "make *our* purpose," "*we* shall be call'd purgers." Throughout the monologue, Brutus explicitly refers to the group of conspirators in the third person, asserting the collective nature of the scapegoating:

> Let's be sacrificers but not butchers, Caius.
> We all stand up against the spirit of Caesar,
> And in the spirit of men there is no blood;

11. Burkert et al., *Violent Origins*, 73–74.
12. Burkert et al., *Violent Origins*, 74.

> O that we then could come by Caesar's spirit,
> And not dismember Caesar! But, alas,
> Caesar must bleed for it! And gentle friends,
> Let's kill him boldly but not wrathfully;
> Let's carve a dish fit for the gods,
> Not hew him as a carcass fit for hounds;
> And let our hearts, as subtle masters do,
> Stir up their servants to an act of rage,
> And after seem to chide 'em. This shall make
> Our purpose necessary, and not envious.
> Which so appearing to the common eyes,
> We shall be call'd purgers, not murderers.[13]

The scapegoating mechanism can also be found in race and class conflicts. In 1964 during the era of the Civil Rights Movement, poet, playwright, and civil rights activist LeRoi Jones (later known as Amiri Baraka) wrote a one-act play entitled "The Dutchman." In the story, a thirty-year-old white woman named Lula and a twenty-year-old African-American man named Clay ride a New York city subway train. Lula torments Clay, mocking him and setting up verbal and psychological traps, caricaturing him according to racial stereotypes examples. Lula pushes the process of victimization to its limits. Jones the playwright dramatically uses Clay as a representative of often-scapegoated Black peoples and Lula as a representative of all the white victimizers, painting an historical portrait of Blacks at a pivotal point of the Civil Rights Movement.

In their study on "The Dutchman" in *Black Theatre USA: Recent Period 1935-Today*, the critics write:

> Lula sets out to seduce Clay, but to accomplish this she must first mold him into the image that she desires—the stereotypical Black figure whom whites create and demand. She taunts Clay about those things that single him out as middle-class, igniting his anger. Lula eventually discovers that gentle, "complaisant" Blacks can also be threatening and dangerous.[14]

Eventually, after having played out all the power games on her victim, Lula murders Clay. Finishing the sacrifice, she has two passengers dispose of the body. But not content with the sacrifice of one Black man, Lula resumes her position in the subway car and turns her gaze upon another young Black

---

13. Girard, *Shakespeare*, 212, cited from Shakespeare, *Julius Caesar* (II.i.162–80).
14. Hatch and Shine, *Black Theatre USA*, 381–82.

The Sacrificial Crisis and the Scapegoat Mechanism

man who has just stepped in. The cycle begins again—the campaign of racial cleansing and dehumanization continues, Jones suggests.

Jones's play may be read as a commentary on the *all-against-one* attacks against the Black community for asserting its power throughout the Civil Rights Movement. Black people were still arbitrarily being lynched up until those times. Ralph Ginzburg's *100 Years of Lynchings*, a critical study of antiblack mob violence from the late nineteenth century to the mid-twentieth century, relates newspaper accounts that reveal the scapegoat mechanism at work:

> Headlines in newspapers from around the country have described the horrors of lynching from the late nineteenth until the twentieth century:
>
> "Two Blacks Strung Up: Grave Doubt of their Guilt," "Negro Lynched to Avenge Assault on White Woman," "An Innocent Man Lynched," "Despite Protests of Rape Victim's Parents," "Doubt Bludgeoned Negro Was Accoster of Girls."[15]

Girard even uses the term "lynching" frequently to describe the scapegoating process. There's no doubt that racial and other minorities have often served as scapegoats for the majority.

OUT OF SCAPEGOATING COMES THE PILLARS OF CULTURE

The killing of the scapegoat ends the sacrificial crisis, and order and "peace" return to the community. But matters don't end there. Out of the scapegoat, **culture** is born. According to Girard, the sacrificial crisis produces three outcomes or by-products: **myth, prohibition** (sometimes called taboo), and **ritual**.

Myth. Having survived the chaos of the sacrificial crisis and witnessed its resolution through the sacrifice of an innocent victim, the community comes to believe that the victim *was* indeed responsible for the crisis. This strong belief in the victim's guilt and power to generate a crisis, the story the community tells itself about these events that mystifies them, Girard calls myth.

---

15. The citation from Hatch and Shine's anthology (*Black Theatre USA*, 382) derives from Ralph Ginzburg's *100 Years of Lynching*.

Prohibition. In order to prevent the crisis from occurring again, the community prohibits any imitation of the victim's actions. It proclaims: "Let's not repeat what the victim did, because re-enacting the victim's actions will cause the same destruction the victim previously brought upon us." As Girard points out, the community decides "not to repeat any action associated with the crisis, to abstain from all mimicry, from all contact with the former antagonists, from any acquisitive gestures toward objects that have stood as causes or pretexts for rivalry."[16] This negative proclamation becomes a law to be strictly observed throughout the community: here we have prohibition or taboo.

Ritual. In time, the community comes to view the victim as a quasi-divine hero/god of great power. In order to try to possess and corral the power the victim/hero/god supposedly possessed—power which was on display during the mimetic crisis—paradoxically *some* of the actions of the victim are selectively imitated and repeated symbolically, thereby establishing a ritual.

While prohibition forbids imitation of the victim to forestall further violence, ritual requires strict imitation under certain controlled circumstances, trying to replicate the positive outcomes of the original crisis. This creates a new class of victims designated for that specific purpose. Who are these "new victims"? Girard discusses them in ancient times at length in *Violence and the Sacred*:

> The city of Athens prudently kept on hand a number of unfortunate souls, whom it maintained at public expense, for appointed times as well as certain emergencies. Whenever some calamity threatened—plague, famine, foreign invasion, or internal dissension—there was always a *pharmakos* [ceremonial victim] at the disposal of the community . . . the victim is considered a polluted object, whose living presence contaminates everything that comes in contact with it and whose death purges the community of its ills—as the subsequent restoration of public tranquility clearly testifies. That is why the *pharmakos* was paraded about the city. He was used as a kind of a sponge to sop up impurities, and afterward he was expelled from the community or killed in a ceremony that involved the entire populace.[17]

---

16. Girard, *Things Hidden Since the Foundation of the World*, 28.
17. Girard, *Violence and the Sacred*, 94–95.

The Sacrificial Crisis and the Scapegoat Mechanism

The *pharmakos* or ceremonial victim replicated the characteristics of a previous victim who, upon sacrifice, had successfully resolved the mimetic crisis infecting the community. Before their expulsion or murder, the community nourished and maintained the *pharmakoi* in a location isolated from itself until they could be sacrificed in the same manner as the original victim. This suggests that certain classes or types of people can function as a pool of ready-made scapegoats in a society. Further on, Girard draws out the similarities between the *pharmakos*, medication and those who are qualified to administer it: "It is not surprising that the word *pharmakon* in classical Greek means both poison and the antidote for poison, both sickness and cure—in short, any substance capable of perpetrating a very good or very bad action according to the circumstances and the dosage. The *pharmakon* is thus a magic drug or a volatile elixir, whose administration had best be left by ordinary men in the hands of those who enjoy special knowledge and exceptional powers—priests, magicians, shamans, doctors, and so on."[18]

Scapegoating has existed from the beginning of human history. Indeed, Girard believes it's what makes us human. We're constituted by mimetic desire, after all, and mimetic desire sometimes leads to the scapegoat mechanism. At this point you may be thinking that scapegoating represents a tragic flaw in the human species, the root cause for injustice and the most unspeakable crimes committed against our fellow human beings. And so it is—but it must also be emphasized that, for all the bloodshed it has unleashed, Girard believes the scapegoat mechanism has also been the primary means of averting the complete and total annihilation of humanity. Throughout human history, it's operated as a fail-safe mechanism, pulling societies back from the brink of the destruction of full-out undifferentiated mimetic crises, preventing peoples from tearing themselves apart in a frenzy of unchecked violence. If it hadn't been for the scapegoat mechanism, the lives lost in the chaos of war and social and political upheaval would have been far greater than they were. Without it, humanity might not have survived.

But we can't be complacent, especially now that we understand this mechanism. We must ask ourselves: Can we do better? How can we escape the vicious cycle of scapegoat sacrifices? Is there an alternative to collective violence for dealing with human conflict? If so, what is it, and how can we apply it?

18. Girard, *Violence and the Sacred*, 95.

How Violence Works

So far we have listened to ancient and modern cultures. With one voice, they seem to say, "The victim is guilty." Is that true? Maybe the unanimity can begin to crack. We have looked at our contemporary society, which seems to tell us, teasingly, "You can't always get what you want." Are we trapped by our insatiable desires? For answers, let's look next at what Girard says about mythology and the Bible. He suggests there's another story, another answer to our personal and social crises. Our quest for wisdom is only getting started.

FOR REFLECTION

Now before we move on, let's apply what we've learned in this chapter.

- Have you found yourself singling out a person or group that you didn't know well or at all for criticism? If so, why did you criticize the person or group? What action did you take in word or deed (if any) against this person or group and what was the outcome?

- Let's reverse the question. Have you ever found yourself defending a person or group being targeted for unfair attacks? Have you ever witnessed or been the target of baseless, unjustified attacks and accusations? Think of a time when you were being persecuted and what you did about it?

- During the pandemic, many people dealt with the long-term isolation and separation from friends and family by choosing to establish better relations with them via telephone, video, and other means of communication. Did you experience this constructive side of mimetic contagion and search for community during the pandemic? Did you reach out to and imitate others in ways that were helpful?

- How does mimetic theory account for the scale of violence we see in today's global conflicts?

- Why do you think dictators are successful at creating scapegoats and convincing the multitude to sacrifice them?

5

"And the Solution Is: Sacrifice 'Em"
Myth

UP TO THIS POINT we've discussed mimetic desire in varied forms and how it often leads to doubling, metaphysical desire, and contagion culminating in the mimetic crisis. We've looked at a lot of different examples and texts, some from popular culture, films, and some well-known literary works. Maybe you've recognized yourself or your life-situation in some of these examples. Maybe they have raised compelling questions for you. Many find the ideas of René Girard eye-opening: once you've seen these patterns he describes, you may start to see them everywhere and how they structure and function in our world.

Next we're going to delve into an in-depth analysis of world mythology. As Girard developed his theories, he moved from his initial discoveries in literary works to the study of anthropology and myths from diverse cultures all over the world. As he studied myths, he came also to study the Hebrew Bible and the narratives of the New Testament, expecting to find similar patterns. He was surprised to find important parallels, but also some crucial differences, between myths and the texts of the Bible. In the next three chapters, we'll talk about each of these in turn.

In broadly comparing mythology and the Bible we might initially think that the Bible and biblical stories represent nothing but another set of myths and cultural stories. This simple reasoning, however, falls apart the moment we examine the role of scapegoats and their role in the stories, and how the Bible treats scapegoats. In both myths and in biblical narratives we can easily locate the scapegoating mechanism; however, in mythological texts, Girard noticed that the story is typically told from the perspective of the persecutors, those who create and kill the scapegoat victim. In myth, in other words, they're certain the scapegoat is actually guilty. In these texts, the community unself-critically holds the innocent victim responsible for the plague or contagion and crisis of undifferentiation. If the victim is always guilty according to the persecutors/victimizers, then mythological logic says the scapegoat needs to be sacrificed or expelled to end the crisis. In the eyes of the community, the arbitrary "culprit" has caused the plague and must be sacrificed or expelled.

In the Bible, on the other hand, Girard found the opposite is true: while the biblical texts do depict scapegoating, they instead reveal and denounce the scapegoating mechanism and subvert it as an unjust sacrifice. Siding with the perspective of the scapegoat and the victimized, the Bible proclaims the innocence of the victim. Expanding on this basic, but crucial, difference, Girard highlights the inability of a mythological text to portray the victim's innocence:

> Let us suppose, now, that a myth is an account of scapegoating narrated from the viewpoint of the persecutors. Can this myth inform us that its scapegoat is really innocent, that he was chosen more or less at random, or for reasons completely alien to the misdeed he supposedly committed? Can such a text advertise the scapegoat status of its own scapegoat? Certainly not.[1]

Within the logic of myths, the crowd approves the mob violence against the scapegoat—they see it as required for peace and order to be reestablished. The biblical texts on the other hand, resist and subvert tales of scapegoating and the sacrificing of victims, and the biblical God sides with the victims/scapegoats to establish their innocence, defending them and denouncing the scapegoating mechanism responsible for the violence and sacrifice.

Girard claims the Bible as the first and single most comprehensive text in human history to fully reveal the scapegoating mechanism, but also to denounce it. For him, this revelation alone sets the Judeo-Christian Scriptures apart from mythological narratives. We can see the Hebrew Bible's revealing and denouncing of the scapegoating mechanism, and it's highlighting of the innocence of the victim, as a *sacred* revelation. Up until Genesis, the first book in the Hebrew Bible, Girard stresses, there were no

---

1. Burkert et al., *Violent Origins*, 79.

"And the Solution Is: Sacrifice 'Em"

narratives, mythological or not, that had illuminated and condemned the violence inherent in scapegoating.[2]

EXPEL THE BLIND KING

Let's examine this difference between myth and the Bible further, looking in detail at two well-known, key archaic myths from ancient Greece that reveal the extent of this difference: *Oedipus the King* by Sophocles and *The Bacchae* by Euripides. We can find clear illustrations of the mimetic crisis and how it functions in classical Greek drama in Athens in the fifth century BCE. Focusing on conflicts between *humans and humans* or between *humans and gods*, ancient Greek myths provide ample examples of mimetic themes, sacrificial crises, and acts of sacrifice to resolve them. Perhaps one of the most well-known myths of Western literature, culture and mythology, *Oedipus the King* was written by Sophocles in 427 BCE. In the beginning of this play, Sophocles reminds the reader that Oedipus has defeated the sphinx who rules the city of Thebes. In return, the city of Thebes has granted to Oedipus both the widowed queen, Queen Jocasta, as his wife, and the throne itself, making him the king of Thebes.

The play opens to reveal Thebes in another crisis—this time a terrible plague. The crowd and their priest are searching for a remedy. Oedipus, "whom all men call the Great" emerges, inquiring why the crowd has gathered in front of his palace in such a turmoil. Reaching out to satisfy the crowd, Oedipus listens to the priest who reiterates the horrors of the plague ravaging Thebes. At the end of his plea on behalf of the plague-ridden citizens of Thebes, he asks Oedipus to save their city.

---

2. Although late in his writing, Girard does compare the Bible to a partial unmasking of sacrifice in the Hindu Upanishads. See Girard, *Sacrifice*.

Oedipus and the Sphinx (1864)
Gustave Moreau, French

Oedipus responds by pronouncing that he has already taken action: he has sent Creon—Jocasta's brother—to Apollo's Pythian temple to learn by what "word or action" he could save Thebes. Creon returns to report that the citizens of Thebes need to "purge" and "purify" the city,

> By banishing a man, or expiation
> of blood by blood, since it is murder guilt
> which holds our city in this destroying storm.[3]

3. Sophocles, *Oedipus the King,* 100–102.

"And the Solution Is: Sacrifice 'Em"

Facing this puzzle handed down by the gods at Delphi, Oedipus embarks on finding who murdered the previous king, King Laius. Based on his meticulous search and questioning throughout the city, it soon becomes apparent that Oedipus *himself* had unknowingly murdered Laius in the past. In calling on Creon to discuss the matter with the gods and discussing it himself with the blind prophet, Tiresias, Oedipus finally learns that Laius was his father, and that Jocasta, Oedipus's new wife, is actually his birth mother. A physical defect—a swollen ankle—identifies Oedipus as the murderer of the King of Thebes. This defect he acquired as a child when his parents gave him away to be killed in order to prevent a prophesy—one which warned that Oedipus would kill his father and marry his mother.[4]

Sophocles's tragedy ends with Jocasta hanging herself and Oedipus blinding himself. He places his two daughters, Antigone and Ismene, in Creon's care and then asks Creon to banish him from Thebes, but Creon denies Oedipus's request and instead Oedipus has to return to the palace against his will. This ancient tragedy shows us several key points about mythology and scapegoating:

- Archaic myths explain any natural or supernatural unexplainable effects such as the plague in Thebes in *Oedipus the King* through mythological stories involving various gods at work;

- The myth represents a person, or persons, accused of being the culprit and responsible for the plague as a victim or a god. The plague in Thebes has nothing to do with Oedipus or anyone else in the city, yet mythological logic and reasoning needs to place the blame on a random individual. This arbitrarily chosen victim then becomes the scapegoat for the plague-ridden community;

- In selecting the scapegoat, the community remains unaware of the victim's innocence, but firmly believes that their expulsion or sacrifice will resolve their plague. In the case of Oedipus, he was banished and secluded away from the community.

Sometimes victims in myth are killed, but other times they are expelled from the community. In discussing *Oedipus The King*, Girard points out that the scapegoating in the play does not necessarily need or use mob action: "In the Oedipus myth, there is no physical violence, there is no mob,

---

4. Seen as the "father of psychology and psychoanalysis," Freud is known for using literature as a basis for his psychological theories. Freud utilized *Oedipus Rex* to coin his famous term "Oedipus complex."

the hero is not killed. But the king who replaces him banishes him from Thebes. The citizens are unanimous in their horrified rejection of Oedipus, and Creon acts in their collective name when he pronounces Oedipus's sentence."[5] Oedipus also mutilates himself by tearing out his own eyes, a self-imposed violent act before his expulsion.

Other Greek myths also show tales of violence, vengeance, and the sacrifice of a scapegoat to appease a community's crisis. Another well-known tragedy, *The Bacchae* by Euripides written in 422 BCE, explicitly shows the complete cycle of the mimetic crisis, including the sacrificial crisis. This myth, which centers on Dionysus, the god of wine, and Pentheus, the king of Thebes, takes the reader from an initial conflict created by mimetic desire to the creation of doubles, to mimetic contagion, to the final selection and sacrifice of the scapegoat.

FROM DESIRE TO SCAPEGOATING AND SACRIFICE: THE MIMETIC CYCLE

Seen through the lens of mimetic desire, *The Bacchae* reflects six distinct dimensions of the mimetic crisis that define the birth and resolution of a social or national conflict. We can find all the following:

- The identification of an object of desire (o) by a subject (s) and a model/mediator (m);
- The formation of doubles through desire of this same object, through the mechanism of double mediation;
- The contagious infection and spread of the desire for the object, moving from doubles to the rest of the community as in a contagious plague;
- The contagion ultimately leading to the creation of undifferentiation and the sacrificial crisis;
- The unanimous *all against-one* accusation against the victim-scapegoat;
- The sacrifice of the scapegoat to end the crisis and restore the community to its peace and normal state.

---

5. Burkert et al., *Violent Origins*, 81.

"And the Solution Is: Sacrifice 'Em"

This trajectory of desire—from its inception between a subject and model and an object of desire, to its final violent stages and conclusion of scapegoating and sacrifice—gives us the full mimetic cycle.

As a myth, *The Bacchae* presents its readers with mimetic elements right from the first scene when Dionysus, the god of wine, enters the city of Thebes. The stage directions describes him as "of soft, even effeminate, appearance," and to further emphasize his feminine attributes, Euripides adds that "his face is beardless; he is dressed in a fawn-skin and carries a thyrsus (i.e., a stalk of fennel tipped with ivy leaves). On his head he wears a wreath off ivy, and his long blond curles ripple down over his shoulders." From this description we can see that Dionysus enters the city with an already established undifferentiation in his identity between *man/god* and *man/woman*. The inhabitants of Thebes don't suspect or receive any hints about his real identity, his deadly powers, or supernatural abilities as a god. In addition to disguising himself as a woman, he enters the city wearing a mask. The mask suggests an "all knowing god" that smiles at the future prospects of the city—a foreshadowing of the horrific future for the inhabitants/victims, but an amusing one for the god.

Upon arrival, Dionysus announces his identity and heritage, positioning himself as both one of the gods *and* as a habitant of Thebes. Additionally, while speaking to the audience, he admits to his disguise:

> I am Dionysus, the son of Zeus,
>   come back to Thebes, this land where I was born. [...]
> And here I stand, a god incognito disguised as man[6]

While this opening sequence of Dionysus's homecoming in disguise could be a purely theatrical element, for the reader familiar with the mimetic crisis and the scapegoat mechanism, Dionysus's return in disguise looks not so much like a theatrical device, but as a warning and foreshadowing of the crisis ahead. Though disguised, Bacchus (another name for Dionysus), announces that he is indeed a bearer and creator of chaos through undifferentiation.

---

6. Euripedes, *Bacchae*, 1–4.

Head of Dionysos (The God of Wine and Divine Intoxication) (fourth to fifth century) (Pakistan, ancient region of Gandara)

As we witness the women/chorus following him singing and dancing, mesmerized by his trance, we see the mimetic contagion has already begun. Justifying his appearance to them, Dionysus recounts to the crowd his journey home to Thebes. He describes his conquests and victories in which he used his Bacchic rites to initiate and spread his rituals through a contagion:

> . . . and so along all Asia's swarming littoral
>   of towered cities where Greeks and foreign nations,
>   mingling, live, my progress made. There
> I taught my dances to the feet of living men,
>   establishing my mysteries and rite
> That I might be revealed on earth for what I am:
>   a god.[7]

Looking at the language closely, the words "mingling" and "live" make it evident that the Bacchic spell behaves much like a plague—the god inspires a live and contagious phenomenon. Additionally, we learn that Dionysus doesn't differentiate between nations: his frenzy affects both "Greeks" and the "foreign," revealing a global infection. The contamination of the

---

7. Euripedes, *Bacchae*, 17–19.

conquered nations fully manifests once the population has been initiated to the Bacchic sacred dances, mysteries, and rites.

Dionysus has a strategy for his conquest. He spreads his rites and rituals throughout Thebes, first affecting the female population:

> This city, first
> in Hellas, now in shrills and echoes to my women's cries,
> their ecstasy of joy.[8]

Consumed by ecstasy, the women gather at the mountaintop, clothed in fawn-skin and armed with shafts of ivy in their hands. The description shows us a mob of women dressed and ready for attack and war. Dionysus stops the commotion and addresses his audience again, pronouncing his motive for coming back: to defend his honor from slander spoken by his mother's sisters against his mother, Semele. They committed slander against her by refusing to believe she had slept beside the god, Zeus. Dionysus continues:

> Because of that offense
> I have stung them with frenzy, hounded them from home
> up to the mountains where they wander, crazed of mind,
> and compelled to wear my orgies' livery.
> Every woman in Thebes—but the women only—
> I drove from home, mad.[9]

With the women infected by the Bacchic frenzy, Dionysus has set in motion the irreversible undifferentiation and the sacrificial crisis in Thebes.

Shortly after Dionysus's arrival, Pentheus, the king of Thebes, appears and begins immediate rivalry over power with the god. Pentheus finds Dionysus to be a "stranger" and questions him about his identity, but Dionysus refuses to answer. Pentheus has "the stranger" bound and imprisoned. In rivalry for power, Dionysus warns Pentheus of his divinity, but not believing a word, Pentheus humiliates him by cutting off his blond curls and confiscating his wand. Then to secure the safety of his prisoner, Pentheus confines Dionysus to the palace. The mimetic rivalry between the two continues, with Dionysus warning Pentheus of the consequences of his actions:

> I give you sober warning, fools:
> place no chain on *me*.[10]

---

8. Euripedes, *Bacchae*, 20–21.
9. Euripedes, *Bacchae*, 33–35.
10. Euripedes, *Bacchae*, 503.

Pentheus, caught up in the web of rivalry, discards the warnings and continues with the competition, insisting on his rank and power as the king of Thebes. Rejecting the superiority of this stranger, Pentheus continues to dictate: "But I say: chain him. And I am the stronger here."[11] The attendants exit with the captive Dionysus. Not withholding his godly powers, Dionysus soon calls out for an earthquake and thunder to come and "shatter the floor of the world." The power struggle between human and god creates doubling between Pentheus and Dionysus, which exasperates the emerging sacrificial crisis. This culminates in Dionysus bringing upon Thebes the destructive plague—the earthquake.

Having survived the earthquake's destruction, Pentheus meets Dionysus amongst the ruins of the palace and in a state of confusion asks Dionysus how he escaped the chains. Again, Dionysus responds by alluding to his godliness and divine powers. Still trapped and blind by mimetic rivalry and his sense of kingly pride, Pentheus remains unconvinced. In a moment of oscillating violence, Pentheus chooses to continue with the power rivalry over who controls the city, indicating that Dionysus won't escape his anger. Vengeance now becomes the aim and vocabulary of both doubles.

As the power rivalry continues, a messenger announces that the women of Thebes have been caught in a frenzy—a violent mimetic contagion with strange ritualistic behavior including dancing, drinking and tearing to pieces all the men who come near them. Fascinated, Pentheus decides to see the frenzy first-hand. Though still rivaling one another, events take a turn when Dionysus offers to guide Pentheus to the mountaintop chaos.

Wearing his smiling mask—a symbol of the fact that he's the one behind the crisis of undifferentiation in Thebes—Dionysus instructs Pentheus to dress as a woman. To humiliate Pentheus further and avenge himself, Dionysus places a wig with long curls on Pentheus's head, completing the transformation and lack of differentiation between them. Pentheus asks Dionysus to lead him "through the heart of Thebes, / since I alone of all this city, dare to go"[12] to which Dionysus ironically responds, "You and you alone will suffer for your city."[13]

We will see how Dionysus will lead Pentheus to the frenzy with this proclamation, invoking the language of *all-against-one*. Once in the frenzy,

---

11. Euripedes, Bacchae, 504.
12. Euripedes, Bacchae, 961.
13. Euripedes, Bacchae, 963

"And the Solution Is: Sacrifice 'Em"

Pentheus will become the sacrifice torn to pieces by the crazed female mob, including Pentheus's mother, Agave.

While Euripides's *The Bacchae* fully illustrates the mimetic cycle—from initial mimetic desire to scapegoating to the final sacrifice—the myth also sheds light on the nature of contagion: namely, when the sacrificial crisis is at work, the crowd thrives and grows on the energy of its own mimetic desire and contagion. The participants in the mob of a mimetic contagion can shift suddenly from just slightly mimetic to an undefeatable sacrifice-hungry mob. Members of the infected group or crowd will close off their previously open circle to protect and strengthen their unanimous desire. In writing about the phenomenon of crowd behavior, Elias Canetti illuminates four aspects of the crowd:

> 1. *The crowd always wants to grow.* There are no natural boundaries to its growth. . . . 2. *Within the crowd there is equality.* This is absolute and indisputable and never questioned by the crowd itself. It is of fundamental importance and one might even define a crowd as a state of absolute equality. A head is a head, an arm an arm, and differences between individual heads and arms are irrelevant. It is for the sake of this equality that people become a crowd and they tend to overlook anything which might detract it. . . . 3. *The crowd loves density.* It can never feel too dense. Nothing must stand between its parts or divide them; everything must be the crowd itself. . . . 4. *The crowd needs a direction.* It is in movement and it moves towards a goal. The direction, which is common to all its members, strengthens the feeling of equality. A goal outside the individual members and common to all of them drives underground all the private differing goals which are fatal to the crowd as such. Direction is essential for the means that it will accept *any* goal. A crowd exists so long as it has an unattained goal.[14]

Far from being unpredictable in its motives, psychology or movement, the crowd resulting from mimetic contagion in Euripides's *The Bacchae* closely mirrors Canetti's description. The mob of women, already gathered and united on the mountaintop, quickly begins to (1) desire to expand with no limitations imposed; (2) gain strength through the equality created by the absence of leaders other than Dionysus himself; (3) remain together in a confined area on the mountaintop before then spreading across Thebes; and (4) become intently focused on the defeat and sacrifice of the rival Pentheus. The crowd dissipates once they attain this goal.

14. Canetti, *Crowds and Power*, 29.

The Bacchic frenzy doesn't limit itself to human sacrifice, but festivities depicted in the play include

> a single woman with bare hands
> tear[ing] a fat calf, still bellowing with fright,
> in two, while others clawed the heifers to pieces.[15]

Realizing the potential danger of this Bacchic frenzy, Pentheus compares the violence to a spreading fire or plague:

> Like a blazing fire
> this Bacchic violence spreads.[16]

Reacting to the violence with violence of his own, Pentheus orders an attack against the crowd of frenzied women, the Bacchae. Dionysus retaliates by giving Pentheus a second chance:

> You have done me wrong,
> and yet, in spite of that, I warn you once
> again: do not take arms against a god.
> Stay quiet here.[17]

Rivalry oscillates in a vicious circle: Pentheus threatens to imprison Dionysus once again; Dionysus responds by suggesting that Pentheus should offer a sacrifice to the god; Pentheus, blind to the impending reality of his own doom, makes an ironic proposal as an answer:

> I shall give your god the sacrifice
> that he deserves. His victims will be his women.
> I shall make a great slaughter in the woods of Cithaeron.[18]

Savoring his revenge on Pentheus, Dionysus, persuades Pentheus to dress up in disguise as a woman, preparing him for the sacrifice that lies ahead. But Pentheus remains unaware he *himself* will be the sacrifice. Hesitant about the trip, Pentheus asks:

> But how can we pass through the city without being seen?
> The god uses the opportunity to declare himself as a guide:

---

15. Euripedes, *Bacchae*, 737–738.
16. Euripedes, *Bacchae*, 777.
17. Euripedes, *Bacchae*, 788–891.
18. Euripedes, *Bacchae*, 796–798.

"And the Solution Is: Sacrifice 'Em"

To which Dionysus responds:

> We shall take deserted streets.
> I will lead the way.[19]

Taking Dionysus's advice to ponder "whether to go to the celebration or not," Pentheus disappears to his palace to reflect about his options. Dionysus, knowing well the laws of desire, pretends not to care so as to further fan the desire he has ignited in Pentheus. With Pentheus inside his palace, Dionysus addresses his female followers, referring to Pentheus as a "prey" caught in "the net" which they have thrown. The choice of the word "net" used in various Greek myths, dramas and tragedies points to the concrete level of sacrificial violence in its final stages—the scapegoat will be caught in a net without any way out, ready to be sacrificed.

Dionysus leads Pentheus through the city to his fate. To launch the sacrifice, Dionysus bends down the highest branch of a fir and, much like a sling, sits Pentheus on it and releases the branch. Pentheus falls amidst the women and Dionysus gives the initiated ones the command to fall upon him:

> Women, I bring you the man who has mocked
> At you and me and at our holy mysteries.
> Take vengeance upon him."[20]

With these words, Dionysus's violence becomes manifest. Rather than protecting Pentheus from war and vengeance, his own purpose is war and vengeance. The vengeance process and how it is carried out reflects the classic mode of scapegoating, the *all-against-one*, by means of stoning the sacrificial victim:

> ... And when they saw my master
> perching in his tree, they climbed a great stone
> that towered opposite his perch and showered him
> with stones and javelins of fir, while the others
> hurled their wands.[21]

Agave, Pentheus's mother, leads the collective act of sacrifice initiated by Dionysus, who like a "priestess with her victim, fell upon him [Pentheus] first." After they rip Pentheus's body apart and toss it across the battle ground, all in the crowd become calmed and appeased. The reference to

---

19. Euripedes, *Bacchae*, 839-40.
20. Euripedes, *Bacchae*, 1079-1081.
21. Euripedes, *Bacchae*, 1094-1097.

Agave being "like a priestess" highlights that the sacrifice of the victim in this Bacchic ritual was already a part of an established ritual of the ancient Greeks. In another reference it's mentioned that Agave, lost in a Bacchic "spell," carries the head of her son, Pentheus, without being aware of what she is doing. The stage directions clearly and boldly state:

> (*Enter Agave with other Bacchants. She is covered with blood and carries the head of Pentheus impaled upon her thyrsus.*)

In archaic religions and mythological texts, things like trance, spell, magic, or voodoo tend to explain the psychological and physical sacrificial phenomenon we see represented there. The Bacchic trance in *The Bacchae* illustrates the deity of wine casting his spell on the population to initiate them into a sacred ritual of sacrificing a victim. The brutal Bacchic spell enacts the worst possible of all punishments: undifferentiation between all participants of the rite, even extending to the victim's mother. Entering the city with the chorus before her, Agave refers to the head on her thyrsus (a sharp pointed implement) as the head of a hunted lion. She's actually proud of her hunted prey as she explains to the chorus:

> Happy was the hunting. . . .
> The whelp of a wild mountain lion,
> and snared by me without a noose.
> Look, look at the prize I bring.[22]

As in all mimetic contagions, the victims are too entranced under the mimetic influence to know any better: one must be outside of the circle of mimetic contagion, uncontaminated by the contagion, to see the reality of the situation. In this case, Cadmus, Agave's father, enters the scene untouched by Dionysus's spell and he proves clear-headed enough to find and identify the dismembered body of Pentheus. Cadmus gives his account:

> Old Theiresias and I,
> had returned to Thebes from the orgies on the mountain.
> before I learned of this atrocious crime
> my daughters did.[23]

The reference to a pre-sacrifice orgy continues to flesh out the nature of the hedonistic god of wine. Cadmus tells of finding several of the mothers and

---

22. Euripedes, *Bacchae*, 1171–1175.
23. Euripedes, *Bacchae*, 1221-1223.

wives who participated in the Bacchic ritual on top of the mountain, referring to them as "still stung with madness" while Agave, "still possessed," made her way back to Thebes.

Agave, through her father's insistence, finally comes out of her Bacchic possession and realizes the head she has been carrying all along was none other than the head of Pentheus, her son. To add to the tragedy one last stroke of punishment, Dionysus exiles Agave from Thebes in expiation for the murders she committed and transforms Cadmus and his wife into serpents. The god's revenge becomes complete.

We have witnessed savage scenes in these plays. The ancient Greek tragedies, Sophocles's *Oedipus the King* and Euripedes's *The Bacchae* give us dramatic examples of archaic myth in which the victim is guilty. They're just two well-known examples of countless myths of this type. The stories are unapologetically violent, told from the perspective of the crowd of persecutors who justify their scapegoating action. In our next two chapters, we'll turn to biblical narratives that tell a very different story even while depicting scapegoating.

FOR REFLECTION

- The tragic story of Oedipus is well-known, partially because it was used by Freud to promote his theories. What is your reaction to Oedipus accepting blame for the plague ravaging the city and tearing his eyes out? Does he seem guilty to you? Is there any reason to doubt how the myth presents his guilt?
- What is your response to the disturbing tale of *The Bacchae*? Is it hard to relate to or does it remind you of some "lynching" you have seen in modern life?
- Have you read any modern stories or seen any films that remind you of the treatment of the scapegoat in ancient myths? How is their treatment of the scapegoat different?

6

From Scapegoats to Deliverance
Episodes from Genesis and the Hebrew Bible

THE PREVIOUS CHAPTER ILLUSTRATED the prominence of the scapegoating mechanism in archaic mythology. Let's now turn to the Hebrew Bible to understand how, in contrast to mythology, scapegoats and the scapegoating mechanism appear there. Although the Bible depicts scapegoating, it also denounces it. In the book of Genesis alone, the first book of the Hebrew Bible, we can find many narratives that reveal the way the scapegoat mechanism works and how it's subsequently subverted by the God of the Bible. To examine the different episodes, Girard breaks them down into three categories of narratives based on: 1) the crisis of undifferentiation; 2) the scapegoat and the scapegoating mechanism; and 3) the birth and promotion of prohibition and rituals to control violence within the community. We've already seen these various themes at work in archaic mythology, but now we'll see how the Bible treats them differently.

In his discussion of myth and the Bible, Girard asserts the similarity of the stories in the Bible and myths in various world cultures: "If I insist first of all the similarities, it is to demonstrate clearly that I am not embarrassed by them, and I am not trying to spirit them away. There can be no doubt that the first books of the Bible rest upon myths that are very close to those found all over the world."[1] Yet, he also notes, "I believe we are dealing with mythic forms that have been subverted but still retain . . . many of the characteristics of myth. If we had nothing but these particular texts, we

---

1. Girard, *Things Hidden Since the Foundation of the World*, 144.

would not be able to stress the radical singularity of the Bible *vis-à-vis* the mythological systems of the entire planet."[2] Now let's look at these ambiguous texts and see where they take us.

ADAM AND EVE IN THE GARDEN STORY

We start with one of the best-known stories in the history of the world. In the creation narrative at the start of the Genesis, Adam and Eve in the garden of Eden are free to eat the fruit of any tree of the garden, except "the tree of the knowledge of good and evil." Additionally, God tells them if they eat from it, they will die. Now the snake which was "the most cunning of all the wild animals the Lord God had made" tempts Eve to eat from the fruit from the tree of knowledge of good and evil, asking her if God really meant they would die if they ate from that tree. Eve answers truthfully: "We may eat of the fruit of the trees in the garden; but God said, 'You shall not eat of the fruit of the tree that is in the middle of the garden, nor shall you touch it, or you shall die.'"[3] (This prohibition may have been made to protect Adam and Eve, not just threaten them with punishment for an arbitrary sin.) The snake, proud and envying God, responds and says to Eve, "You will not die; for God knows that when you eat of it your eyes will be opened, and you will be like God, knowing good and evil."[4] Note that this is the serpent's perspective, born out of rivalry with God. Eve gives into temptation. She desires what the snake proposes to her, taking the serpent as her model instead of God, and eats from the tree: "So when the woman saw that the tree was good for food, and that it was a delight to the eyes, and that the tree was to be desired to make one wise, she took of its fruit and ate; and she also gave some to her husband, who was with her, and he ate."[5]

Right away, in this scene from the third chapter of Genesis, we already find mimetic desire at work: The model/mediator becomes the serpent, the subject is Eve and the object is the forbidden fruit of the tree of good and evil. The snake convinces Eve to break the prohibition placed by God in the garden of Eden, go against God's command, and eat from the fruit of the tree. Furthermore, after having succumbed to the temptation of the serpent,

---

2. Girard, *Things Hidden Since the Foundation of the World*, 154.

3. Gen 3:2–3. New Standard Revised Version (NRSV) of the Bible. Here on all references and quotations are taken from NRSV Bible.

4. Gen 3:4–5.

5. Gen 3:6.

she shares the fruit with her husband, Adam. He too gives in and eats from the forbidden fruit, taking her as a secondary model. Girard points to the negative model the serpent provides: "The Serpent in the mimetic theory of desire is a symbol, an image, of the mediator.... He is therefore, the one who directs the subject towards the bad desire."[6]

After this collective trespassing of Adam, Eve and the serpent, God expels the three from the garden. Though this might initially seem an act of vengeance against them, it's better to understand Adam and Eve's act of collective transgression as the first moment of collective violence of *all against God* found in the Bible. In fact, at the same time as the expulsion of Adam and Eve, God takes the violence upon himself by *not* punishing them with death, which was to be the result of eating the fruit. Girard notes this transference of violence in the first two books of the Hebrew Bible: "In every one of the great scenes of Genesis and Exodus, there exists a theme or a quasi-theme of the founding murder of expulsion. Obviously, this is most striking in the expulsion from the Garden of Eden; there God takes the violence upon himself and founds humanity by driving Adam and Eve far away from him."[7]

THE FOUNDING MURDER AND THE STORY OF CAIN AND ABEL

Exiled from the garden of Eden, Adam and Eve conceive two sons: Cain and his brother Abel. Again, we have a well-known story—the story of the first murder in the Bible. Cain is a farmer and Abel a shepherd. We're told that at the time of offering, Cain brings an offering to the Lord "from the ground," whereas Abel brings the "fatty portion of the firstlings of his flock." The text also says that the Lord God looks favorably upon Abel's offerings, whereas not so with Cain's. As a result of this difference, envy enters the human scene. Cain envies Abel, takes him out to the field, and murders him.

The biblical account of Abel and Cain plays out much like the Roman myth of the twin brothers, Remus and Romulus, in which Romulus's murder of Remus leads to the creation of the city and culture of Rome.[8] The difference between the biblical account and the Roman myth lies in the portrayal of mimetic envy and rivalry: the same dynamic of rivalry

6. Robinson, "Interview with René Girard."
7. Girard, *Things Hidden Since the Foundation of the World*, 142.
8. Girard, *Things Hidden Since the Foundation of the World*, 146–47.

between the two brothers seems to appear in both accounts except that early on, in the foundation of a civilization and city in the Roman myth, mimetic envy does not appear. In the biblical account, the mimetic dynamics of envy and rivalry are made explicit: Abel "kept flocks," whereas "Cain worked the soil;" Cain "offers fruits of the soil" to God as his sacrifice, while Abel offers the "fat portions from his firstborn flock." The difference of the two offerings creates envy between the two brothers as the God of the Bible is represented as accepting the offerings of Abel but not those of Cain. As a result of this envy towards his brother, Cain murders Abel, in what Girard refers to as a **founding murder** that marks the start of human civilization:

> The theme of the founding murder is not only mythical but also biblical. We find it in the book of Genesis, in Cain's murder of his brother, Abel. The account of this murder is not a founding myth; it is rather the biblical interpretation of all founding myths. It recounts the bloody foundation of the beginnings of culture and the consequences of this foundation, which form the first mimetic cycle narrated in the Bible.[9]

According to Girard, this founding murder in the book of Genesis serves a dual purpose. On an immediate level it serves as the representation of the first foundational murder in all of human history, mythology, and literature, but even more importantly, it acts as the "biblical interpretation of all [other] founding myths." In fact, the story recounts the birth of culture and the destructive mimetic cycle itself. As with Adam and Eve's transgression, Cain's murder doesn't go unpunished, as the God of the Bible calls out to Cain:

> And the Lord said, "What have you done? Listen; your brother's blood is crying out to me from the ground! And now you are cursed from the ground, which has opened its mouth to receive your brother's blood from your hand. When you till the ground, it will no longer yield to you its strength; you will be a fugitive and a wanderer on the earth."[10]

---

9. Girard, *I See Satan Fall Like Lightning*, 83.
10. Gen 4:10–13.

**Cain murdering Abel (plate 2 from The Story of Cain and Abel) 1576
Joseph Sadeler I Netherlandish**

Yet God also protects Cain:

> ... Then the Lord said to him, "Not so! Whoever kills Cain will suffer a sevenfold vengeance." And the Lord put a mark on Cain, so that no one who came upon him would kill him.[11]

Note that here alongside the representation of a founding murder, God places a prohibition *against* murder. Girard notes the significance of this event: "Abel is the first in a long line of victims whom the Bible exhumes and exonerates: 'The voice of thy brother's blood crieth unto me from the ground.'"[12] Although Cain and Abel may be the first rivaling brothers, throughout the Bible we will see other brothers who are also trapped by mimetic envy and rivalry, and in some cases, even transformed into doubles.

---

11. Gen 4:15.
12. Girard, *Things Hidden Since the Foundation of the World*, 149.

From Scapegoats to Deliverance

THE HEBREW GOD AND COLLECTIVE VIOLENCE IN NOAH'S STORY AND THE TOWER OF BABEL

Following the same pattern of denouncing violence and taking sides with the innocent and the scapegoats, a third episode in Genesis, the story of Noah, again illustrates the collective violence of a community—against God and itself—on a much larger level. This time, it's the entirety of the Earth that pits itself against God: "Now the earth was corrupt in God's sight, and the earth was filled with violence."[13] Again, in this account with Noah's narrative, we find the crisis of undifferentiation presented to us through metaphors and myths focused on the fall of civilizations. The story is so well known by many of us as we learned it as children. God decides to destroy all this corrupt life on earth, but before doing so, he asks Noah, the last righteous man, to build an ark in which he and his family and a pair of each animal, one male and one female, could embark to avoid the annihilating flood and the end of civilizations. God's flood puts an end to all civilizations because they are so infiltrated by violence, but God ensures that Noah's family and the animals survive the flood in the ark and a new generation begins again. Is this a myth? This ancient story seems mythical in that the whole community is destroyed, and the text seems to indicate that God was responsible. Yet, in contrast to mythology, God is also represented as being good and making sure that the righteous survivors will be saved.

Shortly after the ark settles on a mountaintop, we have a new wrinkle in the story. We are told with time a new generation of nations arises again and they decide to unite and exercise their power by constructing a tower high enough to reach the heavens. God recognizes another crisis of undifferentiation brewing in this human hubris, easily capable of triggering collective violence. In order to prevent these crises and violence between nations and against him, God creates differentiation between the nations:

> Now the whole earth had one language and the same words. And as they migrated from the east, they came upon a plain in the land of Shinar and settled there. And they said to one another, "Come, let us make bricks, and burn them thoroughly." And they had brick for stone, and bitumen for mortar. Then they said, "Come, let us build ourselves a city, and a tower with its top in the heavens, and let us make a name for ourselves; otherwise we shall be scattered abroad upon the face of the whole earth." The Lord came down to see the city and the tower, which mortals had built. And

13. Gen 6:11.

the Lord said, "Look, they are one people, and they have all one language; and this is only the beginning of what they will do; nothing that they propose to do will now be impossible for them. Come, let us go down, and confuse their language there, so that they will not understand one another's speech." So the Lord scattered them abroad from there over the face of all the earth, and they left off building the city. Therefore it was called Babel, because there the Lord confused the language of all the earth; and from there the Lord scattered them abroad over the face of all the earth.[14]

**The Tower of Babel Etching by Anton Joseph von Prenner
(Austrian, Wallerstein 1683–1761 Vienna)**

Once again, in contrast to mythology, here in this episode we see the biblical God acts to create differentiation so as to prevent greater violence and a rising crisis of undifferentiation.

14. Gen 11:1–9.

From Scapegoats to Deliverance

THE LAST EPISODE IN GENESIS: SCAPEGOATING IN THE JOSEPH STORY

A final story from Genesis, the Joseph story, brilliantly illustrates the God of the Bible as a God of love and anti-scapegoating. In this story, the seventeen-year-old youth Joseph tends flocks with his brothers. Born to his father Israel in his late age, Israel (previously known as Jacob, but God changed his name after his struggle with God[15]) makes Joseph a fancy "aristocratic" robe and favors him over his brothers. This special robe and their father's favoritism creates envy among his brothers. Unaware of his brothers' envy, Joseph recounts to them two of his visionary dreams, both of which demonstrate his superiority over his eleven brothers.

Joseph's dreams feed his brothers' envy to the point that they decide to kill him and throw his body in a well. Joseph seems on his way to being set up to be the scapegoat in the story. Of the brothers, though, only Reuben does not accept the planned murder, but instead tries to rescue Joseph:

> They saw him from a distance, and before he came near to them, they conspired to kill him. They said to one another, "Here comes this dreamer. Come now, let us kill him and throw him into one of the pits; then we shall say that a wild animal has devoured him, and we shall see what will become of his dreams." But when Reuben heard it, he delivered him out of their hands, saying, "Let us not take his life."[16]

Joseph's dreams feed his brothers' envy to the point that they decide to kill him, and at Reuben's request the brothers decide instead to sacrifice a surrogate victim—a goat—and smear the goat's blood on Joseph's robe before showing it to their father to make it seem as if Joseph was killed by a wild animal. In Reuben's attempt to rescue Joseph, the others strip Joseph of his robe (the original object of envy) and throw him in an empty cistern. However, unbeknownst to Reuben, Joseph is sold to an Ishmaelite caravan on its way to Egypt, so when Reuben returns to the cistern, he doesn't find Joseph.

---

15. Gen 32:23–28.
16. Gen 37:18–21.

**Joseph Telling His Dreams 1638
Rembrandt (Rembrandt van Rijn) Dutch**

The narrative continues with Joseph's scapegoating in Egypt. At the start things seem to go well, as Joseph is sold to Potiphar, Pharaoh's captain of the guard, and he lives in his Egyptian master's house where God makes him prosper. Seeing Joseph prosper, Potiphar gives him additional responsibilities in the house. But Joseph undergoes scapegoating a second time when Potiphar's wife repeatedly asks Joseph to sleep with her and Joseph refuses:

> And although she spoke to Joseph day after day, he would not consent to lie beside her or be with her. One day, however, when he went into the house to do his work, and while no one else was in the house, she caught hold of his garment, saying, "Lie with me!" But he left his garment in her hand, and fled and ran outside. When she saw that he had left his garment in her hand and had fled outside, she called out to the members of her household and said to them, "See, my husband has brought among us a Hebrew to insult us! He came in to me to lie with me, and I cried out with a loud voice; and when he heard me raise my voice and cry out, he left his garment beside me, and fled outside." Then she kept his garment by her until his master came home, and she told him the same story, saying, "The Hebrew servant, whom you have brought among us, came in to me to insult me; but as soon as I raised my voice and cried out, he left his garment beside me, and fled outside."[17]

Upon Potiphar's return, she repeats the accusation of sexual impropriety to her husband. Believing his wife's accusation, Potiphar throws Joseph into the king's prison, completing the second scapegoating. In prison, however, God once again sides with Joseph and allows him to gain favor from the prison's warden, including allowing him to interpret the dreams of two court prisoners.

Meanwhile, while Joseph is in prison, Pharaoh has two dreams no one can interpret. Upon hearing about Joseph's ability to interpret dreams, Pharaoh liberates him and brings Joseph to court to interpret his dreams. Joseph says that the two dreams are the same; they both indicate a crisis looming in the form of a seven-year period of famine following prosperity throughout Egypt. Joseph adds that the repetition of the dream indicates God is firm about his decision to allow this to happen. Hearing Joseph's interpretation, Pharaoh appoints him to be his right-hand man, enabling Joseph to save food during the seven years of prosperity, distribute it during the famine, and share all Pharaoh's power and authority (but not his title and rank).

The narrative takes a different turn when Israel, faced with the prospect of famine, asks his sons to go to Egypt to buy grain. He requests that his other favorite youngest son Benjamin be kept behind, the sons honor their father's request, and they set off for Egypt. When they arrive, they bow down to Joseph (who they do not recognize) before asking to buy grain. When he

17. Gen 39:10–18.

realizes he is incognito, Joseph cleverly initiates a "staged scapegoating" as an object lesson by accusing his brothers of being spies. The brothers plead their innocence, reaffirming that they have come to Egypt only to buy food. The ten brothers then tell Joseph about their youngest brother, Benjamin, who at the request of their elderly father, was kept at home. Withholding his decision about their "crime," Joseph places his brothers in custody for three days and demands to see their younger brother, Benjamin, before they can be released and given grain.

Fearing God's anger at his false accusation (the "staged scapegoating" of the ten being spies), Joseph releases his brothers from imprisonment but continues to demand the presence of Benjamin in Egypt. To ensure his demand is fulfilled, he keeps one of the brothers, Simeon, as a hostage and gives grain to the rest, with the agreement that failure to bring back Benjamin will result in Simeon's death. He then orders all their bags be filled with grain and that their silver, brought as payment, be placed back in their bags. Joseph's request sets up the scene for a second "staged scapegoating" of the brothers who once scapegoated him.

During their journey back, the brothers realize their silver has been returned to them. Arriving at their father's house, they recount their entire journey to him. The father Israel is distraught about the prospect of having Benjamin taken to Egypt. But Reuben vouches for Benjamin's safety and the nine brothers return to Egypt, this time with Benjamin, to buy more grain.

Upon arrival, Joseph is delighted to see Benjamin. His welcome, however, creates only discomfort and anxiety among the brothers as they fear being taken as slaves as punishment for the silver placed back in their bags. They protest again that they are innocent. Simeon is brought out to them and they're all taken back to Joseph's house where, still not revealing his identity, he asks about their old father. After this, he blesses Benjamin and retreats privately to weep.

Following his warm welcome, Joseph creates yet another "staged" scapegoating by filling his brothers' sacks as before, but this time, he places his own silver cup in Benjamin's sack. Having left the city, Joseph calls on his steward to complete the "staged scapegoating":

> When they had gone only a short distance from the city, Joseph said to his steward, "Go, follow after the men; and when you overtake them, say to them, 'Why have you returned evil for good? Why have you stolen my silver cup? Is it not from this that my lord

From Scapegoats to Deliverance

drinks? Does he not indeed use it for divination? You have done wrong in doing this."[18]

In face of the new false accusations, the brothers defend themselves, adding that should the cup be found among them, the guilty one can be executed for the crime and the rest be taken as slaves. The "staged scapegoating" succeeds. Benjamin is found to have the cup, declared guilty, and the remaining brothers have to agree to be slaves in the court. Reaching Joseph's house, Judah offers to take the blame for Benjamin instead. The substitution would enable Benjamin to be freed and go back to their father, while all the rest of the brothers would have to remain as slaves in Joseph's court. Joseph's staged scapegoatings bear fruit by repeating the violence of their original scapegoating toward him and linking their uncomfortable situation to their own violence.

Joseph won't accept Judah's offer of substitution for Benjamin's execution. He reverses the proposal by saying he now wishes to keep Benjamin as a slave and set the rest free. Judah, however, finds himself caught in an impasse: unable to face their father without Benjamin, Judah reminds Joseph (who they still don't recognize) that their elderly father who would be losing both his two youngest, favorite sons—Joseph and Benjamin. Further, Judah tells of Israel's despairing reaction to Joseph's request about taking Benjamin to Egypt before giving food to the rest of the brothers. Judah's account of his father's grief finally breaks Joseph:

> Then Joseph could no longer control himself before all those who stood by him, and he cried out, "Send everyone away from me." So no one stayed with him when Joseph made himself known to his brothers. And he wept so loudly that the Egyptians heard it, and the household of Pharaoh heard it. Joseph said to his brothers, "I am Joseph. Is my father still alive?" But his brothers could not answer him, so dismayed were they at his presence.[19]

Witnessing his brothers' fear, Joseph asks them not to be afraid but to come close to him. For Joseph, the moment he reveals his identity to his brothers, he becomes their equal. The significance of whether his brothers had scapegoated him, or he his brothers, whether he was their master, or they his servants, dissipates at the moment of his saying, "I am Joseph." Following this revelation, Joseph consoles his brothers by telling them of his past years

18. Gen 44:4–5.
19. Gen 45:1–3.

in Egypt. His brothers react in fear and throw themselves at Joseph's feet, but Joseph responds in a gracious and generous manner reminding them he's in this place because of God's design. All this God intended for good:

> Then his brothers also wept, fell down before him, and said, "We are here as your slaves." But Joseph said to them, "Do not be afraid! Am I in the place of God? Even though you intended to do harm to me, God intended it for good, in order to preserve a numerous people, as he is doing today. So have no fear; I myself will provide for you and your little ones." In this way he reassured them, speaking kindly to them.[20]

Having explained the providential nature of his own scapegoating and his courtly status in Egypt, Joseph extends a generous invitation to his father, brothers and family to join him in Egypt.

> "Hurry and go up to my father and say to him, 'Thus says your son Joseph, God has made me lord of all Egypt; come down to me, do not delay. You shall settle in the land of Goshen, and you shall be near me, you and your children and your children's children, as well as your flocks, your herds, and all that you have. I will provide for you there—since there are five more years of famine to come—so that you and your household, and all that you have, will not come to poverty.' And now your eyes and the eyes of my brother Benjamin see that it is my own mouth that speaks to you. You must tell my father how greatly I am honored in Egypt, and all that you have seen. Hurry and bring my father down here."[21]

Joseph's brothers embrace him, and weeping with him, they reconcile.

When the brothers arrive at their father's home in Canaan, they immediately tell their father of their discovery of Joseph—he is alive and in a position of power in Egypt. The news stuns the disbelieving Jacob. At first he doesn't accept his sons' good news until they recount the story in full and relate Joseph's message to him. Embracing the good news revives Israel's spirit. He exclaims: "Enough! My son Joseph is still alive. I must go and see him before I die."[22] The story has a happy ending, with everyone saved and no one scapegoated anymore.

The Joseph story concludes the book of Genesis. The story clearly portrays scapegoating on multiple levels: (1) the scapegoating of Joseph

---

20. Gen 50:18–21.
21. Gen 45:9–13.
22. Gen 45:28.

by his brothers; (2) the scapegoating Joseph suffers while he is in Egypt; (3) Joseph's two rounds of "staged scapegoating" when he finally meets his victimizer brothers in Egypt during the famine; and (4) the last encounter in which Joseph could continue staging another scapegoating, but instead chooses to reveal his identity, forgive his brothers and save them, their families, and his father from the famine.

The ending of the Joseph story portrays God as a providential presence—one who takes the worst circumstances, trials and scapegoating and turns them, according to the divine will, into a condition that benefits and delivers the innocent and persecuted. Some have thought the Joseph story as a strange way to end Genesis.[23]

However, this final story in Genesis gives us strong reinforcement of the numerous depictions of God undermining and rejecting scapegoating found throughout the entire book. It's therefore the perfect conclusion as commentary about the scapegoating mechanism. Looking at the book of Genesis alone, we can see a clear difference between the gods of mythology and archaic religions such as we saw in *Oedipus the King* and *The Bacchae* in contrast with the God of the Bible. Archaic gods freely allow and even promote scapegoating and the sacrifice of victims, while the biblical narratives make no qualms about denouncing the scapegoating mechanism. Communities may gang up, *all-against-one*, against innocent victims, but the God of Bible is represented as intervening to defend, rescue and deliver them, redeeming the situation.

THE BOOK OF JOB

The revelation of the scapegoating mechanism continues throughout the rest of the books of the Hebrew Bible. In the book of Job, for example, we find Job, another righteous man, accused and victimized by **Satan.** ("Satan" literally means "accuser.") In the story, the figure of Satan acts like a prosecuting attorney wanting to put Job on trial. Some biblical scholars believe we have here an ancient play about the problem of evil. The narrative's prologue introduces us to the idea that Satan's scapegoating of Job before God is a test God allows. Satan challenges God that Job will abandon God if tempted and placed under the most difficult trials. Accepting Satan's challenge, God allows Satan to do as he wishes, *as long as he does not kill Job*. Thus even in the midst of the trial, we can see Job is protected.

23. Goodhart, *Sacrificing Commentary*, 106–7.

> The Lord said to Satan, "Have you considered my servant Job? There is no one like him on the earth, a blameless and upright man who fears God and turns away from evil." Then Satan answered the Lord, "Does Job fear God for nothing? Have you not put a fence around him and his house and all that he has, on every side? You have blessed the work of his hands, and his possessions have increased in the land. But stretch out your hand now, and touch all that he has, and he will curse you to your face." The Lord said to Satan, "Very well, all that he has is in your power; only do not stretch out your hand against him!" So Satan went out from the presence of the Lord.[24]

The ensuing story is brutal. Making the most of the offer, Satan victimizes Job by stripping him to a state of absolute nothingness.[25] He takes away Job's children, gives him ulcers and sores on his body, and makes the once-respected Job become the object of shame. After Satan's intervention, all his neighbors shun Job. Yet during all of Satan's accusations, trials, and attacks, Job doesn't utter a single complaint against God, but remains faithful.

As he is transformed into a victim/scapegoat, three friends join Job and start to give him advice. However, as Girard's book, *Job: The Victim of his People*, points out, rather than being counseled and defended by his friends, Job becomes nothing but a "victim of his people"—a ready-made scapegoat to be bruised, accused and condemned even further. Looking at the text from an anthropological perspective, "Satan's" infliction of suffering and tests may not be so much instances of a literal Satan's actions as a symbolic way of talking about how Job's three friends condemn him. In locating Job as an innocent victim before his three friends, Girard draws out the relation of the scapegoat to their society: a universal relation of all or nothing against the victim where "[t]he scapegoat is the innocent party who polarizes a universal hatred, which is precisely the complaint of Job."[26]

In the rest of the book of Job we see dialogues between Job and his friends in which we find his friends and community—people who once revered and respected him—now accusing and blaming him for his misfortunes. Interpreting the biblical narrative of the book of Job, Girard examines how Job's victimizers are neither really Satan nor the God of the Bible, but rather his society and community.

24. Job 1:8–12.

25. Much like Shakespeare's *King Lear*'s predicament and condition of "having" and "being" nothing in the final acts.

26. Girard, *Job*, 5.

From Scapegoats to Deliverance

Job and His Family (1825–1826)
William Blake, British

As Girard puts it, "He does not say that he has never sinned, he says he has done nothing that deserves his extreme disgrace; just yesterday he could do no wrong and was treated like a saint, now everyone is against him. It is not he who has changed but the people around him. The Job that everyone detests cannot be much different from the man everyone revered."[27]

The dialogues in the book of Job are written in a similar fashion to those in the book of Psalms, both of which explicitly reveal the victim/scapegoat and the scapegoating mechanism. In the book of Job, the dialogues become an interchange where we see Job's friends accusing him, with Job defending himself without uttering a single word against God. In

---

27. Girard, *Job*, 10–11.

the book of Psalms, which uses the form of poetry rather than dialogue, the victims cry out to God for deliverance from their plagued afflictions. As in many of the Psalms where the victim undergoes a long odyssey of victimization and being turned into a scapegoat, the end of the book of Job provides a victorious reward and deliverance for the scapegoat. (This also parallels the Joseph story.) In the book of Job, God himself first speaks and rebukes the "friends" and their perspective on Job as guilty. God then recounts to Job and to all listening the mysteries of creation and reasserts God's sovereignty in all things, even apparent evil and suffering. Second, after a long and epic narrative of gruesome testing by Satan, the Book of Job ends by showing him as victorious and more prosperous than prior to the start of the narrative:

> The Lord blessed the latter days of Job more than his beginning; and he had fourteen thousand sheep, six thousand camels, a thousand yoke of oxen, and a thousand donkeys. He also had seven sons and three daughters. He named the first Jemimah, the second Keziah, and the third Keren-Happuch. In all the land there were no women so beautiful as Job's daughters; and their father gave them an inheritance along with their brothers. After this Job lived one hundred and forty years, and saw his children, and his children's children, four generations. And Job died, old and full of days.[28]

In the end, we find healing in the story. God vindicates the scapegoat of the story and restore him to his place within the community that once rejected him.

PSALM 22

The Psalms are works of poetry in the Bible in which the writer praises or cries out to God, traditionally attributed to King David. Consider the following fragments from Psalm 22. Like Job, the scapegoat in this biblical passage does not utter a single word against God, although s/he cannot find the Hebrew God nor reach him through prayers. We know, however, that God does not abandon the victims/scapegoats, but rather delivers them (verses 1–5). In verses 22:6–8, we find some echoes of Job's complaining and lamenting. Just as with Job, the scapegoat in Psalm 22 may complain and cry out for help but never curses God:

28. Job 42:12–17.

From Scapegoats to Deliverance

> My God, my God, why have you forsaken me?
>   Why are you so far from helping me, from the words of my groaning?
> O my God, I cry by day, but you do not answer;
>   and by night but find no rest.
>
> Yet you are holy,
>   enthroned on the praises of Israel.
> In you our ancestors trusted;
>   they trusted, and you delivered them.
> To you they cried and were saved;
>   in you they trusted and were not put to shame.[29]

Not uttering a curse against God but continuing to exalt God in verses 6–8, the victim compares himself to a "worm," and explicitly points out his scapegoating misfortune for believing in God. The dichotomy between the God of the Bible and the perspective of the accuser/victimizer happens in verse 8 when the scapegoat acknowledges both the victimizers and the biblical God:

> But I am a worm and not human;
>   scorned by others and despised by the people.
> All who see me mock at me;
>   they make mouths at me; they shake their heads;
> "Commit your cause to the Lord; let him deliver—
>   let him rescue the one in whom he delights!"[30]

In the next verses, the scapegoat describes his victimizers as a "pack of villains" encircling him. This encircling the victim serves as a physical reminder of *all-against-one* scapegoating. The resulting sacrifice of the scapegoat leads to "piercing his hands and feet" by his victimizers—an explicit portrayal of the victim's crucifixion by his victimizers. To highlight the crucifixion depicted in the Psalms, the writer draws attention to the victim's shriveled body showing its bones, while the crowd continues to mock the victim and "cast lots for his garment." Seeing his own death by the victimizers, he pleads for deliverance from "the sword," "the power of the dogs," "the mouth of lions" and the "horn of the wild oxen."

> For dogs are all around me;
>   a company of evildoers encircles me.

---

29. Ps 22:1–5.
30. Ps 22:6–8.

> My hands and feet have shriveled;
>   I can count all my bones.
> They stare and gloat over me;
>   they divide my clothes among themselves,
>   and for my clothing they cast lots.
>
> But you, O Lord, do not be far away!
>   O my help, come quickly to my aid!
> Deliver my soul from the sword,
>   my life from the power of the dog!
> Save me from the mouth of the lion!
> From the horns of the wild oxen you have rescued me.[31]

Consistent with a portrayal of the delivering God of the Bible, in the following verses the scapegoat shifts from a plea for the Lord's deliverance to a song of praise, reinforcing the perspective that the Lord has never forsaken the victims and scapegoats, but has heard their pleas:

> For he has not despised or abhorred
> the affliction of the afflicted;
> he did not hide his face from me,
> but heard when I cried to him.[32]

Returning to the power of God, Psalm 22 ends with the affirmation that the God of the Bible *does* hear the voice of the victims and scapegoats. Psalm 22 continues to exclaim:

> Posterity will serve him;
> future generations will be told about the Lord.
>   and proclaim his deliverance to a people yet unborn,
> saying he has done it.[33]

As with the end of Job, the scapegoat victim in this psalm is vindicated and even celebrated, even to a "people yet unborn." The last line of the psalm affirms God's victory: "He has done it."

---

31. Ps 22:16–21.
32. Ps 22:24.
33. Ps 22:30–31.

From Scapegoats to Deliverance
THE SELF-SACRIFICIAL SERVANT OF YAHWEH IN ISAIAH

While many of the biblical Psalms portray the scapegoat and scapegoating mechanism in detail, repeatedly asserting how God never forsakes the scapegoats and the victimized, perhaps no text reaches the full unmasking of violence in the Hebrew Bible as the "Servant of Yahweh" portrayal in the fourth book of the prophet Isaiah, chapter 53.

In discussing the "Servant of Yahweh,"[34] Girard analyzes two different strands of the Hebrew Bible that unveil what he calls "sacred violence" and scapegoating—the first books of the Hebrew Bible and the prophetic texts. As we have seen, in the earliest books of the Hebrew Bible, Girard says, "the founding mechanism [of scapegoating] shows through the text here and there, sometimes strikingly but never completely and unambiguously. The mechanism never gets described as such."[35] But in contrast to the first books, the fragments from the prophetic tradition of the Hebrew Bible provide "a group of astonishing texts that are all integrally related, as well as being remarkably explicit."[36]

In the context of the prophetic texts, Girard focuses on Isaiah 53 versus 2–10 in which the figure of the "Servant of Yahweh" appears during a crisis in order to resolve it. Furthermore, the Servant not only has the characteristic of a human scapegoat of the type we have analyzed but goes further: this victim is one who "as a result of God's own action [becomes] the receptacle for all violence; he takes the place of all the members of the community."[37]

> For he grew up before him like a young plant,
>   and like a root out of dry ground;
> he had no form or majesty that we should look at him,
>   nothing in his appearance that we should desire him.
> ³ He was despised and rejected by others;
>   a man of suffering and acquainted with infirmity;
> and as one from whom others hide their faces
>   he was despised, and we held him of no account.
> ⁴ Surely he has borne our infirmities

---

34. Girard discusses it at length in Book II "The Judeo-Christian Scriptures" of his book *Things Hidden Since the Foundation of the World*, 155–57.
35. Girard, *Things Hidden Since the Foundation of the World*, 155.
36. Girard, *Things Hidden Since the Foundation of the World*, 155.
37. Girard, *Things Hidden Since the Foundation of the World*, 156.

and carried our diseases;
yet we accounted him stricken,
  struck down by God, and afflicted.
⁵ But he was wounded for our transgressions,
  crushed for our iniquities;
upon him was the punishment that made us whole,
  and by his bruises we are healed.
⁶ All we like sheep have gone astray;
  we have all turned to our own way,
and the Lord has laid on him
  the iniquity of us all.
⁷ He was oppressed, and he was afflicted,
  yet he did not open his mouth;
like a lamb that is led to the slaughter,
  and like a sheep that before its shearers is silent,
so he did not open his mouth.
⁸ By a perversion of justice he was taken away.
  Who could have imagined his future?
For he was cut off from the land of the living,
  stricken for the transgression of my people.
⁹ They made his grave with the wicked
  and his tomb with the rich,
although he had done no violence,
  and there was no deceit in his mouth.
¹⁰ Yet it was the will of the Lord to crush him with pain.
When you make his life an offering for sin,
  he shall see his offspring, and shall prolong his days;
through him the will of the Lord shall prosper.

    In this passage, we find an individual with no specific marks or beauty who emerges from a dry wasteland. Rather than being attractive and having "majesty," this figure is perhaps even undesirable. The community has no reason to be attracted to him. In verse 3, his victimhood becomes clear. The community notices his sorrows and suffering and yet they shun him; he is "despised" and "rejected." The language and condition of the victim recalls Job's suffering. In verse 4, the author creates a picture of the self-sacrificial nature of the Servant, as the victim "borne" the community's "infirmities" and "carried out our diseases" while the community considered dismissed him as "stricken," and "struck down by God and afflicted." Referring to verse 4, Girard highlights the fact that instead of God playing a role in the Servant's death, the text suggests it could have been the community's responsibility. Continuing his explication of the last lines of the verse, Girard notes, "yet we esteemed him stricken by God, smitten by him, and afflicted." But it was *not* God at work; "God's responsibility is implicitly denied."[38]

Following the acute observations here in Isaiah of their scapegoat and scapegoating activities, the text represents the community as sacrificing him: he is "wounded for our transgressions," "crushed for our iniquities," by "his bruises [the community] is healed," and most significantly, by "his punishment he made the community whole." Verse 5 clearly indicates a scapegoat who suffered for the transgressions of the community, healed the community "by his bruises" and finally was killed to restore peace to the community, all classic scapegoating steps. In verse 6, the writer highlights two divisions within the community. On one end, the members of the community, like lost sheep, have gone astray; at the same time, the Lord has laid all transgression and iniquity of the community on his Servant, the scapegoat. In verse 7, the writer emphasizes the silent and non-resistant nature of the Servant, where regardless of the pain and suffering imposed on him, he doesn't cry out or "open his mouth," nor participate in any act of violence or speak any deceit:

> [7] He was oppressed, and he was afflicted,
>   yet he did not open his mouth;
> like a lamb that is led to the slaughter,
>   and like a sheep that before its shearers is silent,
>   so he did not open his mouth.

In discussing the Servant of Yahweh, Girard notes the innocence of the victim: "The most striking aspect here, the trait which is certainly unique, is the innocence of the Servant, the fact that he has no connection with violence and no affinity for it."[39] He is not only completely innocent but he has no desire for violence. In verse 8, another unique detail about the oppression and treatment of the Servant of Yahweh is highlighted: he is taken away by force and no one is willing to plead his cause. Equally horrifying is the fact that no one knows where he was taken or "could have imagined his future." Following his arrest, verse 9 reiterates what makes this scapegoat different from the others: though he was innocent, had done no violence or spoken no "deceit" he was buried with the wicked.

---

38. Girard, *Things Hidden Since the Foundation of the World*, 157.
39. Girard, *Things Hidden Since the Foundation of the World*, 157.

In verse 10, we learn that it's the Lord who was the cause of his "suffering." Notice how "Even if the human community is, on several occasions presented as being responsible for the death of the victim, God himself is also implicated by the text as the principal instigator of the persecution."[40] This is a mythological element:

> 10 Yet it was the will of the Lord to crush him with pain.
> When you make his life an offering for sin,
>   he shall see his offspring, and shall prolong his days;
>   through him the will of the Lord shall prosper.

Despite the ambivalence of this portrayal, the end of this fragment once again shows, as with many of the Psalms and the Book of Job, that the God of the Hebrew Bible re-emerges as a merciful God, promising the victim blessings into future generations.

In this passage, the participation of God in Yahweh the Servant's victimage demonstrates that the text still retains some mythological elements. Here, the God of the Hebrew Bible is represented as possibly involved in violence; as benevolent as he has become, we still have here a God capable of vengeance and divine retribution. Viewing the Hebrew Bible as a work of "exegesis in progress," Girard remarks about the ambivalence of the biblical God found in Isaiah's account of the Servant of Yahweh: "Even in the most advanced texts, such as the fourth 'Song of the Servant,' there is still some ambiguity regarding Yahweh . . . in the Old Testament we never arrive at a conception of the deity that is entirely foreign to violence."[41] He continues:

> I think it is possible to show that only the texts of the Gospel manage to achieve what the Old Testament leaves incomplete. These texts therefore serve as an extension of the Judaic Bible, bringing to completion an enterprise that the Judaic did not take far enough, as Christian tradition has always maintained.

Although the Hebrew Bible fully reveals the scapegoat mechanism and gives voice to perspective of the innocent, it still reveals a little ambiguity about God and it doesn't show the resurrection or final vindication of the scapegoat. Continuing with our reading and analysis of the Bible, in the next chapter we'll extend our analysis to the New Testament. There we'll find a continuing extension of the ideas and perspectives present in the Hebrew Bible. So let's next look at how the New Testament, especially the

---

40. Girard, *Things Hidden Since the Foundation of the World*, 157.
41. Girard, *Things Hidden Since the Foundation of the World*, 157.

Gospel texts, represents scapegoats and scapegoating. We've already seen how the God of the Hebrew Bible, Yahweh, and the mythological gods, differ. Do the New Testament and the Gospels, and Christianity itself, shed a new light onto scapegoating and the themes in the Scriptures of the Hebrew Bible? We shall see what Girard says.

FOR REFLECTION

- You may already be familiar with the stories of Adam and Eve, Cain and Abel, and Noah's Ark. What in this reading of these stories gives you new insight into them? Is there anything that surprised you about these stories or Girard's interpretation of them?
- Who do you identify with in the story of Joseph? Why do you think Joseph engages in the "staged scapegoating" episodes with his brothers? Is he trying to teach his brothers a lesson? Make a point about his own innocence once he reveals himself, since they have now also found themselves unjustly accused?
- The story of Job is also well known. What do you think of Job's "friends" and their arguments about his guilt? How do you feel about the end of the book where God vindicates Job? Is this solution to the problem of evil satisfactory to you, or does it fall short?
- Psalm 22 and Isaiah both explicitly present a scapegoat figure and sympathize with the scapegoat's perspective. Can you identify with the speaker of the Psalm? Have you ever felt abandoned? Did anyone recognize your plight or need? How did the situation finally get resolved?

7

The Sacrifice to End All Sacrifices
The Account of Jesus's Passion in the Gospels

NEXT WE COME TO biblical stories of the New Testament which are so well known by many that we may wonder if anything new can be said about them. On the other hand, some may not really know the story of Jesus told in the New Testament, recounted in four separate accounts known as the Gospels (literally meaning "good news.") The Gospel accounts of Jesus's suffering, death on the cross, and resurrection are traditionally called the **Passion**. Crucifixion, the nailing of a criminal on a wooden cross until they died of shock and asphyxiation, was a particularly brutal form of Roman capital punishment. In this chapter, we will look specifically at the Passion narratives (not the whole of Jesus's life) to see what they can tell us about a similarity with myth, but also to show a profound difference. When René Girard first read these familiar texts with his new hypothesis about mimetic desire in mind, he did not expect to find these differences. But they became one of the centerpieces of his thinking because he believes that the Passion narratives fully reveal the scapegoat mechanism once and for all.

First let's review and contextualize our understanding of the connections and contrasts between mythology, the Hebrew Bible, the Gospels. Girard writes:

> To summarize the main point about the Bible and mythology: in the myths an irresistible contagion compels the unanimous communities to see their victims first as guilty and later as divine. The divine stems from their deceptive unanimity of the persecution.

The Sacrifice to End All Sacrifices

> In the Bible by contrast, the confusion of the victimization process and the divine is dissolved and gives way to an absolute separation of the two. As already noted, the Jewish religion no longer turns victims into divinities or divinity into a victim. Monotheism is both the cause and the consequence of this revolution.
>
> Then in the Gospels once again we find not only the first two stages of the mimetic cycle but also the third which the Jewish Scriptures dramatically rejected: the divinity of the collected victim. The resemblances between Christianity and the myths are too close not to awaken the suspicion of a fall back into the mythical.[1]

As Girard noted with the Hebrew Bible, there are some similarities between myths and the stories in the Bible, but also some differences. As seen in chapter 5, myths function by finding a scapegoat on which to blame the newly spreading crisis; then, after designating their victim/scapegoat as the cause of the plague and killing or expelling them, the community elevates them to the stature of a god. The Hebrew Bible refuses this mythological mechanism of divinizing the victim. Against all sacrifices made by humans and the victimizing of the innocent, the biblical God denounces the scapegoat mechanism and comes to save these all too human victims from their victimizers.

We will see how Girard came to believe that the three phases of the mimetic cycle—crisis, scapegoating, and sacred revelation—would be finally and fully completed through the death and resurrection of Jesus Christ. He stresses that he reached this startling conclusion not because he had preconceived ideas about theology at the time of his discoveries, but through his close reading of the texts themselves. Much as he did with the texts of the Hebrew Bible, Girard reads the Gospel texts of the Christian New Testament and sees those texts both reenacting and subverting the patterns of myth, going even further than the Hebrew Bible in their implications.

In a clear formulation of the differences between myth and the Bible, we find that: (1) in mythology and archaic religions the victimage mechanism and scapegoating not only take place, but the victimizers within the myth affirm them; (2) but in taking sides with victims and scapegoats, the God of the Hebrew Bible denounces scapegoating and the victimage mechanism; and (3) further, with the Gospels and New Testament, the texts represent God himself becoming human, in the person of Jesus Christ—and despite his innocence, they show him as being accused and killed as a scapegoat by all factions and groups of people. In other words, we see the

---

1. Girard, *I See Satan Fall Like Lightning*, 121.

all-against-one scapegoating mechanism again, but this time as *against God himself as the innocent victim*. This is a startling development. In the Gospel accounts, Jesus is opposed, abandoned and denounced by all, only to be killed by shameful crucifixion, but he rises from the dead in three days. A small group of his followers see him after the resurrection event and establish the validity of his innocence against the false accusations which caused his scapegoating, false condemnation, and death on the cross. This third and final step—the completion of the revelation depicting the resurrection of Jesus in the four Gospels—makes the New Testament distinctly different from the Hebrew Bible.

Let's look in more detail at the narratives in the Gospels of the events surrounding Jesus's arrest, crucifixion, and resurrection. Over the course of Jesus's Passion account in the Gospels several pivotal themes come to light: (1) the role of the crowd's mimetic contagion and violence unleashed towards Jesus/the victim; (2) the small crowd of Jesus's followers after Jesus's crucifixion and resurrection; and (3) the role of what the Gospels call the *Paraclete*, or Holy Spirit, in defending the victims and assuming responsibility for the resurrection.

IS THE NEW TESTAMENT A MYTH?

For the crucifixion to have the same structure as myth, it has to have a unanimous *all-against-one* victim mechanism. No one person or group of people can be held responsible for Jesus's crucifixion. Virtually *everyone* participates in the violent contagion responsible for Jesus's death, including almost all his apostles (hand-picked inner circle), who flee and betray Jesus by contributing to the sacrificial mob's mentality and actions against him.

Aware of the power of the collective mimetic contagion against him, Jesus warns his apostles of his upcoming crucifixion and resurrection, telling them that they too will fall away from him. Hearing Jesus recount the future news of his Passion, Peter vehemently rebukes Jesus, stating he will never betray him:

> Peter said to him, "Though all become deserters because of you, I will never desert you." Jesus said to him, "Truly I tell you, this very night, before the cock crows, you will deny me three times." Peter said to him, "Even though I must die with you, I will not deny you." And so said all the disciples.[2]

2. Matt 26:33–35.

Defiant and ignorant, the other eleven disciples echo Peter's assertion, behaving mimetically. They aren't capable of fathoming how they could ever fall into the predicted contagion, and they vow to always remain with Jesus. After the disciples' firm affirmation to never disown or deny Jesus, they all move to the garden of Gethsemane, where Jesus wants to pray to God his Father in preparation for his crucifixion. Jesus asks his three favorite disciples, Peter, John, and James, to wait for him, keep watch, and pray while he prays. The disciples fail this small request as they fall asleep three times; Jesus catches them asleep and chastises them. This foreshadows *all* the disciples betraying Jesus once he gets arrested and crucified. In the Gospel of Luke we find the details that he is praying so "earnestly" such that his sweat became "like drops of blood" and an angel appeared to give him strength:

> He came out and went, as was his custom, to the Mount of Olives; and the disciples followed him. When he reached the place, he said to them, "Pray that you may not come into the time of trial." Then he withdrew from them about a stone's throw, knelt down, and prayed, "Father, if you are willing, remove this cup from me; yet, not my will but yours be done." Then an angel from heaven appeared to him and gave him strength. In his anguish he prayed more earnestly, and his sweat became like great drops of blood falling down on the ground. When he got up from prayer, he came to the disciples and found them sleeping because of grief, and he said to them, "Why are you sleeping? Get up and pray that you may not come into the time of trial."[3]

With the three disciples fast asleep, a violent mob armed with swords and clubs pours into the garden to arrest Jesus. Upon the arrival of this mob with Judas, Jesus's betrayer among his followers, Peter instantly decides to defend Jesus and, drawing his sword, he cuts off the ear of the servant of the high priest. In response to this act of violence committed by one of his disciples, Jesus responds by rapidly dispersing the violence. Rebuking his disciple, Jesus emphasizes non-violence against the violent mob: "Then Jesus said to him, 'Put your sword back into its place; for all who take the sword will perish by the sword. Do you think that I cannot appeal to my Father, and he will at once send me more than twelve legions of angels?'"[4]

---

3. Luke 22:39–46.
4. Matt 26:52–53.

The Agony in the Garden (ca. 1652)
Rembrandt (Rembrant van Rijn) Dutch.

In the events that unfold next, Jesus becomes the ultimate scapegoat. Faced with the growing mob, his disciples desert him and flee while the Roman soldiers seize and arrest him. The disciples, infected by the contagion, unwillingly abandon Jesus; earlier they had affirmed their loyalty to him, but now, under the intoxication of the mass contagion, they are swept away. Deserted by his disciples, Jesus is brought before the high priest, Caiaphas, the teacher of the law, and the religious elders, who all interrogate Jesus trying to find false evidence against him in order to put him to death. Under questioning and accusations, Jesus remains silent, until finally the high priest asks him about his identity as the Jewish Messiah, something which

The Sacrifice to End All Sacrifices

he confirms. As Jesus's identity begins to be questioned and accusations freely made against him, Jesus's accusers scapegoat him and treat him as a *guilty* man. Finally, in a clear case of the *all-against-one* pattern, they condemn him for blasphemy, and the high priest and his followers decide Jesus deserves the death sentence. After resolving this, "Then they spat in his face and struck him; and some slapped him, saying, 'Prophesy to us, you Messiah! Who is it that struck you?'"[5]

Meanwhile, as the religious leaders and the crowd actively scapegoat Jesus, the contagion catches up and influences the disciples once again. With the confusion of the crowd and reappearance of the contagion, Peter denies Jesus three times. When asked directly by others if he was with Jesus, he vehemently denies it and pretends to not know him. With the third denial, however, Peter remembers Jesus's prediction and weeps:

> Then he began to curse, and he swore an oath, "I do not know the man!" At that moment the cock crowed. Then Peter remembered what Jesus had said: "Before the cock crows, you will deny me three times." And he went out and wept bitterly.[6]

It would not be until later, after the resurrection, that Peter would become fully aware of his and all the other followers' blindness to the contagion. As Girard notes, "In speaking to the Jerusalem crowd some days after the resurrection, he [Peter] stresses the *ignorance* of those possessed by violent contagion."[7]

By early the next morning, the chief priests and religious elders have decided to put Jesus to death. Binding him as a guilty prisoner, they hand him over to Pilate, the governor and Roman authority in that area. Pilate, despite his authority, quickly becomes a part of the mimetic contagion. Knowing full well that Jesus is innocent and that much of the animosity against him has come from envy,[8] Pilate faces the option of either taking the side of Jesus's innocence or playing into the crowd's desire for his death. Before the ever violent, multiplying crowd, he offers to release another political prisoner named Barabbas, someone who the multiplying crowd had wanted to release by vehemently crying out for his freedom. However, cornered by the contagion and the frenzy of the mob, Pilate agrees to the

---

5. Matt 26:67–68.
6. Matt 26:74–75.
7. Girard, *I See Satan Fall like Lightning*, 191.
8. Mark 15:10–11.

crowd's insistence that Jesus be put to death. Pilate's choice of crucifying Jesus and setting Barabbas free to appease the crowd officially seals the fate of "scapegoat" upon Jesus—he will serve as an innocent unanimously sacrificed to the community.

The mob's unquenched thirst for violence demands that Jesus die by crucifixion, a punishment reserved in Roman society for the lowest of criminals. Even though knowing Jesus is innocent, in face of the shouting and growing mob Pilate hands Jesus over to be flogged and crucified. The soldiers join the frenzy of the crowd by flogging and torturing Jesus—turning him into the guilty one—the *one victim or scapegoat for all*. Following their torture of Jesus, the soldiers force him to carry his cross to Golgotha, meaning "The Place of the Skull," where they post the charges against him on a sign on his cross: "THIS IS JESUS, THE KING OF THE JEWS." Then they crucify him. Upon his death, Jesus gives up his spirit and an earthquake follows with the dead rising from their graves (which in the text signifies a cosmic effect). Finally, Jesus is recognized by others as the Messiah, including by a Roman centurion and those with him keeping guard. "Now when the centurion and those with him, who were keeping watch over Jesus, saw the earthquake and what took place, they were terrified and said, "Truly this man was God's Son!"[9]

After his death on the cross comes Jesus's burial. A rich man named Joseph, who had become one of Jesus's disciples, asks Pilate for Jesus's body. The Gospel text tells us, "So Joseph took the body and wrapped it in a clean linen cloth and laid it in his own new tomb, which he had hewn in the rock. He then rolled a great stone to the door of the tomb and went away. Mary Magdalene and the other Mary were there, sitting opposite the tomb."[10] Upon request from the chief priests and the religious leaders who want his tomb secured, Pilate places a guard on watch by the tomb for three days to ensure that no event of any sort will take place after the crucifixion. Those who wanted the tomb secured are referring to Jesus's prophesy that he would rise three days after the crucifixion: "Therefore command the tomb to be made secure until the third day; otherwise his disciples may go and steal him away, and tell the people, 'He has been raised from the dead,' and the last deception would be worse than the first.'"[11]

---

9. Matt 27:54.
10. Matt 27:59–61.
11. Matt 27:64.

The Sacrifice to End All Sacrifices

Christ Crucified between the Two Thieves: The Three Crosses (1653) Rembrandt (Rembrandt van Rijn) Dutch.

With Jesus abandoned by his disciples and followers, crucified and buried in a tomb, what are we left with in the Gospel account? Thus far, we have no reason to separate, in structure or narrative, any difference between the Gospels and mythology. In fact, the two have so much in common it's hard to differentiate them. We've seen this pattern before. First a crowd forms, then selects a victim as a scapegoat, who is sacrificed in front of the whole community. Those performing the sacrifice consider the victim a deity. We can see that in both mythology and the Gospels we have the same pattern as in the mimetic cycle.

But the story of the death and burial of Jesus doesn't end the Gospels, or for that matter the New Testament. Jesus, called in the text "the lamb of God," has been scapegoated, crucified to death, and buried in a guarded tomb—which makes the narrative seem like it belongs in the realm of mythology. But the biblical text goes on to show Jesus being resurrected within three days and a small group of followers witnessing this with their own eyes. They then go on to proclaim their testimony to the resurrection event, both in writing and in person.

Comparing the crowd accusing the victim in both mythology and the Gospel accounts, Girard exposes a fundamental difference between them: in mythology, the crowd appears unanimously against the single victim—a perfect representation of the *all-against-one* pattern—whereas in the Gospels, the *all-against-one* pattern falls apart, when during the crucifixion, a small faction of Jesus's followers separate from the majority. Unlike the masses, who perceive Jesus as guilty, this small group views Jesus as God. The small group of people who refuse to go along with the contagion and perception of guilt destroys the unanimity or perfect agreement of the crowd. In mythology, such a division can't exist within the persecuting crowd; the crowd must be fully *unanimous*—that is, there must be a complete closure against the victim of *all-against-one* violence—or the scapegoating just doesn't work. Highlighting this fundamental difference between mythology and the Bible, Girard describes how this contrast establishes the uniqueness of the Gospels:

> Moreover, contrary to what happens in the myths, it is not the unanimous mob of persecution who sees Jesus as the Son of God and God himself; it is a rebellious minority, a small group of dissidents that separates from the collective violence of the crowd and destroys its unanimity. This minority group is the community of the first witnesses to the Resurrection, that is, the apostles and those who gather around them. This dissident minority has no equivalent in the myths. Around the mythic deities we never see the community divided into two unequal groups, of which only the smaller one would proclaim the divinity of the god. The structure of the Christian revelation is unique.[12]

We have already seen how the Hebrew Bible rejected the representation of mythological gods who create scapegoats, sacrifice them and subsequently elevate them from a place of guilt to a place of divinity. Expanding on the representation of scapegoats in mythology and the Bible, Girard elaborates on the role of scapegoating in archaic-religions and mythology, Judaism and the Hebrew Bible, and the Gospels.

Girard points out that the Gospels give us a new twist on an old story: with Jesus represented as God himself incarnate in the New Testament, the mimetic cycle gains a third and completed level, which focuses on the divinization of a collective victim. As we've seen, the Gospels show Jesus as a

---

12. Girard, *I See Satan Fall Like Lightning*, 123.

victim of collective violence who is crucified and shortly after resurrected. But here's the new part: the Gospel texts accept the idea of divinity of the victim, and the resurrection serves as the proof of Jesus's divinity and his innocence of all the false accusations and scapegoating everyone witnessed before he was crucified. Standing out as a unique and fundamental aspect of the Gospels and the Christian New Testament, the resurrection account claims Jesus to *be* the same God who defies and overcomes scapegoating and collective violence. In highlighting this unique aspect of the Gospels and the New Testament texts, Girard notes: "Then in the Gospels once again we find not only the first two stages of the mimetic cycle but also the third, which the Jewish Scriptures dramatically rejected: the divinity of the collective victim."[13]

THE RESURRECTION

The account of Jesus's resurrection is included in all four Gospel accounts, with each presenting the resurrection from a different perspective. Let's compare the resurrection narratives in the Gospel of John, the fourth and last gospel, with that of the Gospel of Matthew, the first.

The Narrative of the Resurrection in the Gospel of John

The Gospel of John depicts the resurrection in three parts. In the first part of the narrative, Jesus's followers Mary Magdalene, Peter and John find the tomb empty:

> Early on the first day of the week, while it was still dark, Mary Magdalene came to the tomb and saw that the stone had been removed from the tomb. So she ran and went to Simon Peter and the other disciple, the one whom Jesus loved, and said to them, "They have taken the Lord out of the tomb, and we do not know where they have laid him." Then Peter and the other disciple set out and went toward the tomb. The two were running together, but the other disciple outran Peter and reached the tomb first. He bent down to look in and saw the linen wrappings lying there, but he did not go in. Then Simon Peter came, following him, and went into the tomb. He saw the linen wrappings lying there, and the cloth that had been on Jesus' head, not lying with the linen wrappings but rolled up in a place by itself. Then the other disciple, who

---

13. Girard, *I See Satan Fall Like Lightning*, 121.

reached the tomb first, also went in, and he saw and believed; for as yet they did not understand the scripture, that he must rise from the dead. Then the disciples returned to their homes.[14]

In the second part, the resurrected Jesus appears to Mary Magdalene, asks her why she's weeping, and reveals himself to her and asks her to recount her encounter of the resurrection to the other disciples:

> But Mary stood weeping outside the tomb. As she wept, she bent over to look into the tomb; and she saw two angels in white, sitting where the body of Jesus had been lying, one at the head and the other at the feet. They said to her, "Woman, why are you weeping?" She said to them, "They have taken away my Lord, and I do not know where they have laid him." When she had said this, she turned around and saw Jesus standing there, but she did not know that it was Jesus. Jesus said to her, "Woman, why are you weeping? Whom are you looking for?" Supposing him to be the gardener, she said to him, "Sir, if you have carried him away, tell me where you have laid him, and I will take him away." Jesus said to her, "Mary!" She turned and said to him in Hebrew, "Rabbouni!" (which means Teacher). Jesus said to her, "Do not hold on to me, because I have not yet ascended to the Father. But go to my brothers and say to them, 'I am ascending to my Father and your Father, to my God and your God.'" Mary Magdalene went and announced to the disciples, "I have seen the Lord"; and she told them that he had said these things to her.[15]

In the third part of the resurrection narrative in John, Jesus appears to his followers while they are hiding from persecution from the religious leaders in a room:

> When it was evening on that day, the first day of the week, and the doors of the house where the disciples had met were locked for fear of the Jews, Jesus came and stood among them and said, "Peace be with you." After he said this, he showed them his hands and his side. Then the disciples rejoiced when they saw the Lord. Jesus said to them again, "Peace be with you. As the Father has sent me, so I send you." When he had said this, he breathed on them and said to them, "Receive the Holy Spirit. If you forgive the sins of any, they are forgiven them; if you retain the sins of any, they are retained."[16]

14. John 20:1–10.
15. John 20:11–18.
16. John 20:19–23. Jesus and all his disciples were Jews, so it's wrong to claim that the

The Sacrifice to End All Sacrifices

**The Resurrected Christ Appearing to Mary Madelene in the Garden
South Netherlandish (ca. 1500–1520)**

Jesus is talking here about the Holy Spirit as the same spirit, which was in him all along, one of divine love, the very power of God. The next two lines of the narrative demonstrates the unbelief of Jesus's disciple Thomas: "So the other disciples told him, 'We have seen the Lord.' But he said to them, 'Unless I see the mark of the nails in his hands, and put my finger in the mark of the nails and my hand in his side, I will not believe.'"[17]

Jews killed Jesus, as some antisemitic readings of the Gospel stories have claimed. The text makes it clear that *everyone*, including the Romans, killed Jesus. The disciples here are afraid of the *particular* religious leaders who opposed Jesus in life and condemned him to death.

17. John 20:25.

In the second part of the same scene, the resurrected Jesus appears to Thomas and the other disciples and asks "doubting" Thomas to see and touch the wounds of the crucifixion for himself. At that point, Thomas touches the wounds and recognizes the resurrected Jesus not only as "Lord" but also as "God":

> A week later his disciples were again in the house, and Thomas was with them. Although the doors were shut, Jesus came and stood among them and said, "Peace be with you." Then he said to Thomas, "Put your finger here and see my hands. Reach out your hand and put it in my side. Do not doubt but believe." Thomas answered him, "My Lord and my God!" Jesus said to him, "Have you believed because you have seen me? Blessed are those who have not seen and yet have come to believe."[18]

The Gospel has thus far been extremely detailed in creating a hyper-realistic scene. In the third and last part of the narrative in the Gospel of John, this realism of Jesus's presence continues: having helped his disciples to catch some fish in a miraculous manner, the resurrected Jesus eats grilled fish with his disciples. The final chapter then shows the third time the disciples affirm the resurrection:

> After these things Jesus showed himself again to the disciples by the Sea of Tiberias; and he showed himself in this way. Gathered there together were Simon Peter, Thomas called the Twin, Nathanael of Cana in Galilee, the sons of Zebedee, and two others of his disciples. Simon Peter said to them, "I am going fishing." They said to him, "We will go with you." They went out and got into the boat, but that night they caught nothing.
>
> Just after daybreak, Jesus stood on the beach; but the disciples did not know that it was Jesus. Jesus said to them, "Children, you have no fish, have you?" They answered him, "No." He said to them, "Cast the net to the right side of the boat, and you will find some." So they cast it, and now they were not able to haul it in because there were so many fish. That disciple whom Jesus loved said to Peter, "It is the Lord!" When Simon Peter heard that it was the Lord, he put on some clothes, for he was naked, and jumped into the sea. But the other disciples came in the boat, dragging the net full of fish, for they were not far from the land, only about a hundred yards off.
>
> When they had gone ashore, they saw a charcoal fire there, with fish on it, and bread. Jesus said to them, "Bring some of the

---

18. John 20:26–29.

fish that you have just caught." So Simon Peter went aboard and hauled the net ashore, full of large fish, a hundred fifty-three of them; and though there were so many, the net was not torn. Jesus said to them, "Come and have breakfast." Now none of the disciples dared to ask him, "Who are you?" because they knew it was the Lord. Jesus came and took the bread and gave it to them, and did the same with the fish. This was now the third time that Jesus appeared to the disciples after he was raised from the dead.[19]

Notice how in this passage, we learn even the exact number of fish caught by the disciples in the net. The resurrection accounts in John stress both psychological and physical realism.

The Resurrection in the Gospel of Matthew

In the Gospel of Matthew, the account focuses on the women—Mary Magdalene and the "other" Mary—who visit the tomb after the first day of the week. Matthew tells us an angel descends, rolls away the stone to Jesus's tomb and proclaims the resurrected Christ to the two women. Having announced the news of Jesus's resurrection, the angel asks the women to go to Galilee and share the news with the other disciples. The two women, in fear and joy, head out to Galilee to announce the good news. On the way to Galilee, Jesus suddenly appears before the two women, saying, "'Greetings!' And they came to him, took hold of his feet, and worshiped him. Then Jesus said to them, 'Do not be afraid; go and tell my brothers to go to Galilee; there they will see me.'"[20] Reaching the disciples in Galilee, the two women share the good news of Jesus's resurrection, and soon after, the disciples meet with Jesus once again.

The resurrection is the final event of the Gospel narrative. Jesus is first seen by the two women and subsequently by Jesus's other disciples, affirming the *non-mythical*, but *literal* truth of Christ's divinity to this small group of his followers and subsequently to the rest of the world, through their oral and written accounts. This small group, although lacking prestige and attention from the majority of the community, begins and continues to share the news of the resurrection. Soon, this active minority has the strength to stand up against the unanimity (the *all-against-one* pattern) of

---

19. John 21:1–14.
20. Matt 28:10.

the persecuting crowd that originally crucified Jesus. Observing this phenomenon, Girard writes:

> But on the third day of the Passion the scattered disciples regroup again about Jesus, who they believe is risen from the dead. Something happens in extremis that never happens in myths. A protesting minority appears and resolutely rises up against the unanimity of the persecuting crowd. The latter becomes no more than a majority, numerically overwhelming, of course, but incapable from now on of totally imposing its conception of what has happened, its *mythical* representation on the Crucifixion. . . . The protesting minority is so minuscule, so lacking in prestige, and above all so late in forming that it doesn't affect all the working of the single victim mechanism. However, its heroism will enable it not only to continue to write or be responsible for the writing of the accounts that will spread everywhere the subversive knowledge of scapegoats unjustly condemned.[21]

The question in Matthew now becomes focused on asking how the followers of Jesus, who almost all themselves were crazed and taken by the violent contagion, suddenly have the strength, power and courage to speak against the majority that was still under the influence of the governing dark powers against Jesus. They must have possessed a force greater than the contagion of the collective violence that scapegoated and crucified Jesus.

Comparing stories of collective violence in archaic societies (in which victims were divinized) with Jesus's resurrection and post-resurrection accounts, Girard notes that the effect of the collective violence and scapegoating action was so powerful in those archaic societies that they divinized the violence. In contrast, the Gospel accounts represent the collective violence and scapegoating that led to the crucifixion as of human origin, and furthermore, show that with the resurrection, a power greater than the power of collective scapegoating was at work:

> To break the power of mimetic unanimity, we must postulate a power superior to violent contagion. [If we have learned one thing in this study], it is that none exists on the earth. It is precisely because violent contagion was all-powerful in human societies, prior to the day of the Resurrection, that archaic religion divinized it. Archaic societies are not as stupid as we think. They had good reasons to mistake violent unanimity for divine power.[22]

21. Girard, *I See Satan Fall Like Lightning*, 188.
22. Girard, *I See Satan Fall Like Lightning*, 189.

The Sacrifice to End All Sacrifices

Looking at the resurrection narratives in the four Gospels, they strongly imply the resurrection was possible only through a divine power that could not only overcome the violent contagion and scapegoating process, but also fully save the victim from the power of death. This power resurrected Jesus and enabled his followers to see, hear and touch the resurrected Christ, resuming their place as his followers, this time with full conviction and faith.

In the Gospel of Matthew we find Jesus not only meeting with his followers and disciples but also asking them to convey the news of the resurrection and his teachings to the rest of the world:

> And Jesus came and said to them, "All authority in heaven and on earth has been given to me. Go therefore and make disciples of all nations, baptizing them in the name of the Father and of the Son and of the Holy Spirit, and teaching them to obey everything that I have commanded you. And remember, I am with you always, to the end of the age."[23]

In this command to his disciples, Jesus mentions what Christians will later come to call the divine Trinity, or one God in three persons: the Father, the Son, and the Holy Spirit.[24] Jesus then promises his disciples, "I am with you always, to the very end of the age." What does Jesus's promise to his disciples mean? Jesus is referring to the Holy Spirit who, as the Gospels show, will be descending upon his followers fifty days after his resurrection to empower them.

THE ADVOCATE, LAWYER AND DEFENDER

In the Gospel accounts, it is the Holy Spirit, or the *Paraclete* (the Greek word for the Spirit of God) who defeats the mimetic violence and contagion and brings the resurrection to fruition. Jesus promises to send this living, divine spirit, the third member of the Trinity, to his followers to guide them and prevent them from falling away again in the face of mimetic violence and contagion. Elaborating on the Holy Spirit's importance and crucial role post-resurrection, Girard writes: "The Spirit takes charge of everything. It would be false, for example, to say the disciples 'regained possession of themselves': it is the Spirit of God that possesses them and does not let them

---

23. Matt 28:18–20.

24. In Christianity, God is seen as one in three persons. The Son, who is Jesus, and the Holy Spirit eternally exist with God the Father in a dynamic, loving relation. This one God in three persons is called the Trinity.

go."²⁵ How does the Holy Spirit, who guided and protected Jesus's followers, appear and function amidst victims and victimizers? The Gospels continue to identify and denounce all scapegoating and the *all-against-one* sacrificial mechanism in favor of defending the innocent. In fact, the Greek word given in the Gospel of John for the Holy Spirit, *paraclete* (stemming from the Greek *parakletos*), actually means literally the "lawyer for the defense," the "defender of the accused," the "helper," the "advocate," or the "defender of the innocent and victims." This legal term is the opposite of the spirit of accusation called "Satan," which means "the accuser."

The Passion narratives do vividly illustrate the scapegoating and crucifixion of Jesus on the cross, but then their story continues on three days later when Jesus is resurrected and returns to his family and followers. The miracle of the resurrection of God in human form by the *Paraclete* or advocate, the full vindication of the one who was scapegoated and crucified, establishes, to the select few who saw him, that Jesus was indeed the Son of God—and even was God himself. To this effect, the New Testament affirms:

> We declare to you what was from the beginning, what we have heard, what we have seen with our eyes, what we have looked at and touched with our hands, concerning the word of life [Jesus]—this life was revealed, and we have seen it and testify to it, and declare to you the eternal life that was with the Father and was revealed to us—we declare to you what we have seen and heard so that you also may have fellowship with us; and truly our fellowship is with the Father and with his Son Jesus Christ. We are writing these things so that our joy may be complete.²⁶

Continuing with his discussion of the Holy Spirit, Girard adds: "We should take with utmost seriousness the idea that the Spirit enlightens the persecutors concerning their act of persecution. The Spirit discloses to the individuals the literal truth of what Jesus said during the crucifixion: 'They do not know what they are doing.' We should also think of the God whom Job calls 'my defender.'"²⁷ This "defender" God is the same God of both the Hebrew Bible and the Gospels. But in the Gospels, the victim is revealed to be God himself, and the Holy Spirit fully vindicates and rescues this ultimate victim of violence from death.

---

25. Girard, *I See Satan Fall Like Lightning*, 189.
26. 1 John 1:1–4.
27. Girard, *I See Satan Fall Like Lightning*, 190.

As we have seen, the Holy Spirit or *Paraclete* is another name for the Spirit of God who defends the victims and scapegoats against the collective violence and contagion. The *Paraclete* or *defender/advocate* contrasts with the spirit of Satan (the "*accuser*"). "Satan," which Girard regards as the biblical name for the spirit of mimetic contagion, violence, and the scapegoat mechanism itself, is defeated in the resurrection. When we say that after Jesus's resurrection, the *Paraclete* holds victory over Satan, we are saying that the spirit of mimetic envy, disorder and the scapegoat mechanism has been overcome. Christianity births the triumph of the *Paraclete* over death and Satan, whose name originally means "accuser before a tribunal," that is, *the one responsible for proving the guilt of the defendants* (and thus perpetuating scapegoating). According to Girard, the Gospels hold "Satan" responsible for all mythology told from the perspective of the persecutors. In contrast, the Gospel accounts of Jesus's suffering, death, *and resurrection* become attributed to the power of the Holy Spirit that defends victims unjustly accused.[28]

In conclusion to his discussion of the Holy Spirit within a violent world filled with scapegoating and collective violence, Girard makes the acute remark: "Humankind is never the victim of God; God is always the victim of humankind."[29] The victimization of God, who is perfectly good and wants the best for creation, by humankind appears most visibly in Jesus, an innocent, blameless victim of crucifixion. Fortunately, we can now escape that cruel, mimetic cycle. Girard's interpretation of the Gospel narratives gives us hope and a new perspective impossible before. It becomes possible not only to see scapegoating for what it is, but to choose to live a different way entirely. In the next chapter, we'll return full circle to the themes of mimetic desire we've identified at work in our culture, and look at the choices before us.

FOR REFLECTION

- Are you familiar with the story of Jesus? If so, does this interpretation shed any new light on these well-known stories in the Bible? If you're not familiar with Jesus, can you see the contrast between his story and that of other victims in mythology? How are they similar and different?

28. Girard, *I See Satan Fall Like Lightning*, 190.
29. Girard, *I See Satan Fall Like Lightning*, 191.

- Girard regards "Satan" as a name for the destructive mimetic processes we've discussed throughout this book. It's the power of mimetic contagion and scapegoating which has manifested itself through human history. Does this interpretation make sense to you? Can you relate to this interpretation and see it at work in our world today?
- What do you think of the resurrection narratives? Do the stories of the early followers of Jesus seem plausible (even though supernatural)? Does Girard's interpretation of them help make better sense of them?
- World leaders often talk about "de-escalation" of global conflicts. What do you think brings about effective de-escalation?

Conclusion
The End of Violence

AT THE BEGINNING OF this book we learned what mimetic desire is—we saw how it can be a generative mechanism capable of producing good, but also how it can produce conflicts and violence. It can teach children how to imitate their parents, teach young people how to imitate the top students, athletes, or other "heroes," and it can encourage individuals to imitate peaceful models that they find in life or fiction.

But in the same classroom where some imitate the stellar students, others are envying and rivaling them. In the same school one student can envy another for their trendy shoes, even murdering them to get the shoes. Outside schools, in the neighborhood, adults may imitate and rival their other neighbors ("Keeping up with the Joneses") to try to possess what the neighbor has. We also saw how mimetic desire drives different fashions, marketing, and advertisements, where people imitate and become doubles of one another.

As we've seen, mimetic desire doesn't end with doubles. It searches for different ways to continue. Having created a set of doubles between two individuals, doubles can spread into the community. While doubles erase the differences between two individuals, the spreading of the doubles in the community erases differences between *all* members of the community creating a crisis of undifferentiation. Immersed in a crisis of undifferentiation, the confused and aggravated community feels it needs a sacrifice to restore order back to itself. Here, the scapegoat is born. Unable to solve how the crisis came about, the crowd seizes upon a random individual or group of individuals, blames the crisis on them, and expels or sacrifices them to end the community's crisis of undifferentiation.

What then is the solution to the problem of violence? Violence has been there since the beginning of the world and archaic times and it still exists today. While René Girard never wrote a book or treatise that systematically gave a formal solution for ending violence, we can find clues and guidance regarding a solution in his writings, interviews and books—from his first book, *Deceit, Desire and the Novel*, where he discovered and introduced mimetic desire, to his last book, *Battling to the End*, which he claimed was an "apocalyptic" book, warning us of what would happen if violence is not transcended.[1] By using the word apocalyptic, Girard was not referring to the last book of the New Testament, the book of Revelation, where by some interpretations the end of the human world and civilization would be brought about by God of the Bible. Instead, he was warning us as humans that if we don't take responsibility for our actions and choices, we ourselves (not God) will bring about the end of the world and human civilization. In the introduction to *Battling to the End* he muses that only certain kinds of conservative Christians are typically those who still talk about the end of the world, "but they have a completely mythological conception of it. They think that the violence of the end of time will come from God himself. They cannot do without a cruel God. Strangely they do not see that the violence we ourselves are in the process of amassing and that is looming over our own heads is entirely sufficient to trigger the worst."[2] Despite his apocalyptic vision, Girard's work did not leave us hopeless.

Let's start with his first book, *Deceit Desire and the Novel* (which in the original French is called *Romantic Lies and Novelistic Truths*). In his first book, he tells us about one of his key concepts: *conversion*. The first step that needs to happen to loosen the grip of negative and destructive mimetic desire is for a person to be able to see and recognize it for what it is. Girard calls this process of coming to see a "conversion." This is when novelists eventually are able to see how mimetic desire works and therefore are able to write their novels accurately by depicting negative mimetic desire. The conversion Girard speaks of involves taking on a new point of view in relation to negative mimetic desire; to see how one is enmeshed in it. Girard calls this new way of seeing of the protagonists in the novel a "**novelistic conversion.**" Within the world of the novel, the author sometimes depicts the hero recognizing the lies and influence of negative mimetic desire under which they had been living, allowing them to be able to take on a new point of view, one based on truth and no longer on deception and lies.

---

1. Girard, *Battling to the End*, ix.
2. Girard, *Battling to the End*, xvi.

Conclusion

Girard analyzes the hero *Don Quixote* in Cervantes's novel in *Deceit, Desire and the Novel* before he proceeds to talk about four other authors and their masterpieces of Western literature. We discussed the character of Don Quixote earlier and can see how throughout the entire novel named after him he was under the spell of destructive mimetic desire—he was living a "**romantic lie**." On his deathbed he has a conversion of understanding where he realizes he was living a lie—he sees he's *not* a great knight like his model/hero Amadis de Gaul. Unfortunately, this enlightenment happens late in the novel. Now, lucid and clear about his identity and the world around him, Quixote dictates his will from his bed, renounces his addiction to chivalric romances, and dies. It would have been interesting to see Cervantes write a few more chapters to show how the healed and newly converted Don Quixote would have lived, behaved and acted once free of his illusions and destructive mimetic desire, which made him waste his life on phantoms.

Writing about the great novels and their heroes, Girard discovers how each hero in his literary examples struggles with their life and reality as a result of living under a "romantic lie" and under the influence of negative mimetic desire. The character may experience the pain and mental torture of a false life, but the good news is they can change. After all, Girard points out that the writers themselves have changed in order to be able to show us the truth about desire. We can find their depiction of the workings of mimetic desire, then awakening, realization and conversion not only in novels but also in other art forms such as film and theater, as we have seen in this book. These insightful stories often found in great masterpieces invite us to have a conversion ourselves.

Let's talk further about the nature of the "novelistic conversion." People often think of conversion in relation to religious faith. In Girard's thinking, this connection with faith is relevant but that's not the only meaning of the word. On a biographical note, Girard was born to a Roman Catholic family in France, but he fell away from practicing that faith until he came to the United States and started teaching. In the process of reading and teaching the great novel and writing his first book *Deceit, Desire and the Novel*, he rediscovered his faith and started practicing it. Thus, for him, his insights into the novelistic conversion he speaks about in his first book and his own return to the Catholic faith happened at the same time.

Girard stresses that in the realm of mimetic desire, we are not bound to stay fixated on and be a slave of destructive mimetic desire and the scapegoating mechanism. Like the heroes of great novels and other virtuous or holy people who overcome their shortcomings and the workings of destructive mimetic desire, we too can undergo a conversion. It's important to note that Girard does not necessarily use the term "conversion" in the sense that one has to convert to Christianity. Rather he points out that any true act of conversion involves the adoption of a "transcendent" viewpoint upon mimetic processes. This means being able to see that one has been trapped in the negative imitation of a model and envying others, with all the catastrophic effects this leads to. Girard points out that this can't simply be a rational process but involves a reorientation of one's whole being: "True conversion engenders a new relationship to others and to oneself."[3] This reorientation creates a new self where "[d]eception gives way to truth, anguish to remembrance, agitation to repose, hatred to love, humiliation to humility."[4] Novelistic conversion involves being able to see and name negative, destructive mimetic desire in a way you couldn't before, and repentance for participating in it. But how is this conversion brought about?

We know by now that as humans getting rid of imitation simply isn't possible. Girard stresses this throughout his work. While he discovered, developed, and presented mimetic desire and its various mechanisms in his first books, he continued to test it out and write about it till the very end. Girard continually reminds us that as we are mimetic creatures, not imitating isn't really an option. But he points out that though we can't stop imitating, as we become self-aware we can self-consciously choose good models. We have the freedom to choose once we see what we are doing: "it shouldn't be concluded that it [mimetic theory] denies the existence of individual freedom."[5] There are better and worse forms of imitation. As we have seen, in many situations such as those with parents with children and teachers with students, external mediation with good models can lead to good and positive outcomes for the individual and the culture of which they're a part.

Girard believes that if a person has had good models early in life, they won't be so subject to negative mimetic desire, but instead, they will be able to "move very freely from one model to the next. The movement is natural if one has met the right models in one's formative years."[6] Early experiences

3. Girard, *Deceit, Desire, and the Novel*, 295.
4. Girard, *Deceit, Desire, and the Novel*, 294.
5. Girard, *When These Things Begin*, 124–25.
6. Girard, *Battling to the End*, 133.

Conclusion

with good external mediation may be important in our ability to move from destructive to more constructive forms of mimetic desire or resist negative mimetic desire altogether, because we have internalized good models. We continue to make choices utilizing and expanding their values. In good external mediation we quite openly and self-consciously imitate our hero or model. "To make an effective imitator, you have to openly admire the model you're imitating, you have to acknowledge your imitation. You have to explicitly recognize the superiority of those who succeed better than you and set about learning from them."[7] Of course, we have to pick genuinely superior models or we can fail. It's well known that younger artists learn from those who are older at first by copying their style or approach. Once they've internalized what that mediator has to teach, they move on to a more challenging model, one who can guide them as their own creativity develops.

External mediation is a good start, but it may not be enough as a full-scale solution to the problem of violence. It has its own set of problems. For one thing, it needs distance between the mediator and the subject imitating so that envy and rivalry don't arise. But that's becoming harder and harder in our modern world, where many people can rise in professions, social class, and wealth with education and hard work. Girard points out that a society based mainly in external mediation must be traditional and hierarchical in nature, where the subjects can't attain the material or more intangible objects desired by their models. In the modern culture we live in, however, we no longer experience such a rigidly separated society with different roles and classes of people who naturally don't compete with one another, and so envy, rivalry and violence have become much more common and widespread. Often, if we really put our minds to it, we really can also attain what the boss or a politician or a pop star desires! Beneficial external mediation collapses easily into a more problematic, envious internal mediation, so we get into conflict even with our "heroes." Then, as always happens in internal mediation, we find that even if we manage to obtain the object we vicariously desire, we're left strangely unsatisfied. We try to grasp that elusive something the mediator seems to have that remains just out of reach. That's the nature of what Girard has called metaphysical desire. We are wanting, always wanting. We've all felt this kind of frustration.

A second problem arises as well: in our modern-day democratic society, where we place value on the individual and people try to be free and

---

7. Girard, *When These Things Begin*, 44.

independent, the necessity of external models is often questioned or done away with. For Girard, this is an illusion, part of the "romantic lie." For him, mediators are always there, whether we admit it or not. But he also acknowledges in his last book that though we are imitative beings, for all these reasons mentioned here external mediation no longer works very effectively on a widespread scale in the modern world. Internal mediation is now everywhere, leading to frustration and dissatisfaction, confusion, even and in the worst case scenario the scapegoat mechanism. If that's indeed the case, then what are we to do? Girard says the answer is to imitate the *only type of* model who is capable of drawing close to those imitating without it leading to violence. For Girard, this ultimate model is Jesus Christ.

Girard speaks of Jesus as the only individual capable of withstanding and rejecting violence on all levels. We've seen this in the Passion narratives. Girard highlights this fact when he notes: "Jesus is the only man who achieves the goal God has set for mankind, the only man who has nothing to do with violence and its works."[8] Jesus can be a guide for us, a model immune to participating in violence and its contagion. Because Jesus perfectly imitates the desire of God, which is not a grasping type of desire, we cannot compete with God because God doesn't crave objects of satisfaction. Instead, God loves everyone and is generous to all creation. Jesus offers us here something beyond external mediation: we can become just like him but without rivalry because he can show us how to be like this generous God. He can be the person who shows us the way to love our neighbors as ourselves and even how to love our enemies:

> But I say to you: Love your enemies and pray for those who persecute you, so that you may be children of your Father in heaven, for he makes his sun rise on the evil and on the good and sends rain on the righteous and on the unrighteous.[9]

Jesus gives us a new kind of desire. In his last book, Girard recommends following the example or model of Jesus through what he calls an "**innermost**" or "**intimate mediation**."[10] Innermost mediation means entering into and imitating Jesus's close relationship with a loving God, choosing charity as a way of life. This works itself out in part by refusal to retaliate against one's enemies, something which Jesus explicitly teaches.

---

8. Girard, *Things Hidden Since the Foundation of the World*, 213.
9. Matt 5:44–45.
10. Girard, *Battling to the End*, 133, 158, 169, 205.

Conclusion

Interestingly, Girard points out that novelists who become able to see negative mimetic patterns and accurately depict them through a process of "conversion" are very close to discovering this same religious truth about Jesus. In talking about the heroes of great novels Girard writes, "Repudiation of a human mediator and renunciation of **deviated transcendency** inevitably call for symbols of **vertical transcendency** whether the author is Christian or not."[11] "Vertical" transcendency is a way of talking about becoming oriented toward a reality that is bigger than human destructive mimetic desire, through taking a model who won't inspire envy and rivalry. For Girard, this model is Jesus directly or other "Christlike" or saintly models who love and forgive rather than competing and creating conflict. Discussing conversion and the choice of models, Girard writes:

> As we already explained, conversion means to become aware that we are persecutors. It means choosing Christ or a Christlike individual as a model for our desires. It also means seeing oneself as being in the process of imitating from the beginning. Conversion is the discovery that we have always, without being aware of it, been imitating the wrong models who lead us into the vicious circle of scandals and perpetual frustration.[12]

While "vertical" transcendency can get us out of negative mimetic desire and draw us closer to God or loving relationships, "deviated" transcendency, on the other hand, means remaining stuck in envy and rivalry with those human models which seem to offer the satisfaction of spiritual or transcendent needs, but can never satisfy. As Benoît Chantre points out, "'Deviated transcendence' is measured by the jealous proximity between mediator and subject: democratic culture, which multiplies the number of possible models, also multiplies the risks of rivalry. It is easier and easier to hate, more and more difficult to feel admiration."[13]

But this is not what happens with the best kind of mediator, who desires the well-being of the subject without appropriation or grasping. Put in religious language, we can say that God's relationship to us shows us how to love one another, and is the opposite of, and antidote to, the human tendency to envy, rivalry, and violent contagion. Jesus is such a good model because he most clearly shows a relationship to God (a transcendent reality) that is nonviolent by nature and is loving instead.

11. Girard, *Deceit, Desire, and the Novel*, 312.
12. Girard, *Evolution and Conversion*, 223.
13. Chantre, "Steeple of Combray," 162.

So far, we have talked about the individual, but what about the society and the world? How does Girard and his thought relate and extend to violence on a communal and global level? Is there an alternative to violence? Fortunately, the answer is yes. We have another alternative to the apocalyptic vision of endless sacrifice, what Girard calls conversion away from negative and destructive mimetic desire and toward what Jesus referred to as the **"kingdom of God"**—that is, his invitation to a society devoid of sacrificial violence. This new non-sacrificial reality is possible when people give up all retribution and sacrificial violence and participate instead in a contagious loving reality. How does this work?

As we have seen, the state of doubles locked in mimetic rivalry is a grim one, if not ultimately deadly. One of the two must be sacrificed in order for the doubles to become two separate individuals and entities, unless a "miracle," or an "act of mercy" as Shakespeare calls it, takes place to separate and differentiate them and establish both as two different personas. In *Midsummer Night's Dream*, Oberon has mercy on the sets of doubles by allowing Puck to separate them by the magic potion. A merciful act stops the rivalry, managing to differentiate and save the doubles without any sacrifice.

We face a choice as a society, as a global community. If we don't choose an act of mercy capable of breaking the chain of doubles and turning toward mercy and forgiveness, it will lead from one retribution to another, one sacrifice to another, and one sacrificial crisis to the next. A domino effect takes place with negative and destructive mimetic desire, envy, doubling, retribution, and scapegoating. It's like the ripples in a lake as a drop expands endlessly outward. Today, wherever you look, no matter how you look at it, modern day civilization is trapped in a chain of violence. We all have felt its effects, and we can come to recognize, it—and to change it. Let's now look at how this solution works in two similar scapegoating accounts. For the first story, let's take Shirley Jackson's famous short story "The Lottery"[14]—and for the second, let us take a look at a passage from the Gospel of John, involving Jesus, an adulterous woman and the crowd. The two narratives differ on the immediate level in that the crowd in "The Lottery" takes action, selecting and sacrificing the victim, whereas in the account of Jesus from the Gospel of John the victim is freed, and the situation

---

14. For discussion and analysis of Shirley Jackson's "The Lottery" see chapter 4, pages 54–55.

Conclusion

is resolved in the community through non-sacrificial means. Why are they different?

In Shirley Jackson's horrifying short story "The Lottery," in a seemingly wholesome and normal small town, an unspeakable annual event occurs. We have a story where an arbitrary individual is selected and stoned to death by the *entire crowd*—notice that the crowd has unanimously agreed to participate in the event, even though they themselves may become the victim. Young and old, male and female, all the individuals in the community have each agreed to play their roles and participate in their annual ritual of the lottery. The villagers gather in the month of June, the townspeople draw lots by taking slips of paper out of a black wooden box, and the "winner" is then stoned.

In contrast, in the Gospel of John, we find a story of an adulterous woman, a vengeful crowd threatening death by stoning for her transgression, and how Jesus responds to the situation. (Although the woman in the story appears to be genuinely guilty of adultery, she is still functioning as a scapegoat because she is no more guilty than her partner, who is neither named nor condemned.) Jesus confronts the crowd without any eye contact—which would have only fueled their anger—but instead:

> Jesus bent down and wrote with his finger on the ground. When they kept on questioning him, he straightened up and said to them, "Let anyone among you who is without sin be the first to throw a stone at her." And once again he bent down and wrote on the ground. When they heard it, they went away, one by one, beginning with the elders; and Jesus was left alone with the woman standing before him. Jesus straightened up and said to her, "Woman, where are they? Has no one condemned you?" She said, "No one, sir." And Jesus said, "Neither do I condemn you. Go your way, and from now on do not sin again."[15]

In this second case, Jesus dissipates the accusers and violence, peace is established, and the adulterous woman is set free. The crowd disappears, one individual at a time: from the first one, who is the eldest, to the second, third and so forth until the entire crowd has dispersed.

Jesus's remedy to the crisis of undifferentiation includes everyone in the crowd individually as well as the crowd as a whole. Note that had the first individual chosen to cast a stone, that action would have triggered a mimetic wave and "ripple effect" inviting *all* in the crowd to do the same.

15. John 8:6–11.

But this isn't what happens, because of what Jesus does—because Jesus invites each individual in the crowd to examine their own conscience, to become self-aware. Only if they are innocent themselves, he says, should they cast the first stone. And if they are not innocent themselves, he implies, they should not be condemning and stoning others. In this way he puts them to the test, which makes them uncomfortable. Finally, the first one—the eldest and perhaps the wisest, we might guess—withdraws in an "act of mercy." This creates a positive contagion where others follow. They all individually move away from their threat of participating in collective violence, from the eldest to the youngest (wisest to least experienced). The violent crowd thus disperses. Jesus knows this will happen to interrupt the violent impulses if people are confronted with what they are doing. The account in the Gospels not only serves as a model for peace but it also explicitly demonstrates a non-sacrificial solution to the problem of sacrificial violence.

Jesus's object lesson here in this story is consistent with his explicit teachings elsewhere in the Gospels. In the Gospel of Matthew, Jesus gives the crowd this new teaching:

> "You have heard that it was said, 'You shall love your neighbor and hate your enemy.' But I say to you, Love your enemies and pray for those who persecute you, so that you may be children of your Father in heaven; for he makes his sun rise on the evil and on the good, and sends rain on the righteous and on the unrighteous."[16]

In this way, Jesus calls each to an understanding that everyone is equal before God, who is generous to all. Peace can only be achieved, Girard posits, if the individual and the crowd both adhere to his new "rules" of the kingdom of God individually as well as a community: do not retaliate, but instead love your enemies. Another way of putting it is Jesus's other teaching of "Love your neighbor as yourself"[17] as the second of the greatest commandments, a command first found in the Hebrew Bible.[18] Jesus's precepts and teaching all point to rejecting and refusing to participate in sacrificial violence. He's quite explicit about it. When the religious teachers of the day challenge him for why he accepted having dinner at a notorious tax collector's home, he responds by quoting from Hosea in the Hebrew Bible: "Go and learn what this means, 'I desire mercy, not sacrifice.' For I have come to call not the

---

16. Matt 5:43–45.
17. Mark 12:31.
18. Lev 19:18.

Conclusion

righteous but sinners."[19] Jesus gives us his new non-retributive law of love which replaces the old law of sacrificial retribution, ending violence.

At first glance, Jesus's commands to love and forgive enemies appear counterintuitive and paradoxical. Who would want to obey them? After all, humans often want to take revenge on their neighbors or their neighboring countries. Humans tend to get caught up in violent contagion, seeking to kill, creating ripples of violence, so as to continue to believe in sacrifice in order to practice it. But what seems to be renunciation is really the way to peace: Jesus reforms the law by subverting its sacrificial thrust. Violence can be renounced, as Jesus teaches.

But we can still wonder: How can one individual following the non-sacrificial precepts of Jesus end the community's crises, even the world's crisis? The question is a good one. Can one individual make a difference? The answer is "yes," because the individual can act as a mimetic model for the rest of their community. Ultimately, the community as a whole will need to commit to follow the precepts as well, but this can happen through a chain of positive contagion. In this manner the individual and the community can put a halt to the sacrificial crisis. The implications of this are profound, says Girard, if we could only see it: "For all violence to be destroyed, it would be sufficient for all mankind to decide to abide by this rule. If all mankind offered the other cheek, no cheek would be struck. But for that to be possible, it would be necessary for each person separately and all people together to commit themselves irrevocably to the common purpose."[20] We see this sort of profound "act of mercy" occurring in the story of the woman caught in adultery.

Accepting or rejecting Jesus's invitation to his precepts, which means living according to what the Gospels and Girard call the "kingdom of God" will yield two opposing results: acceptance of the invitation will bring about peace for individuals and the community as illustrated in the story of the woman caught in adultery, and rejection of the invitation will continue endorsing and fostering violence and disorder endlessly, as we see in the scapegoating story of "The Lottery" and so many of the others we have examined. We can either accept Jesus's precepts of the kingdom of God about a new way of living, or reject them. We have before us the choice of two different paths on either side of the abyss.

---

19. Matt 9:13. (First found in the Hebrew Bible in Hos 6:6: "For I desire steadfast love and not sacrifice," the knowledge of God rather than burnt offerings.)

20. Girard, *Things Hidden Since the Foundation of the World*, 211.

The crossing from one side of the abyss that's violent to the other, peaceful side seems impossible; they simply seem too far apart to fathom a possible solution. But concerning the two sides of the abyss, Girard points out that crossing from one side to the other isn't impossible: "Mankind can cross this abyss, but to do so all men together should adopt the single rule of the kingdom of God. The decision to do so must come from each individual *separately*, however; for once, others are not involved."[21] By this Girard means that a choice lies with each individual, to break away from the rest of the crowd. This means stepping back from violent patterns, as we have seen, through recognition or "conversion." The next, seamless step is choosing instead good models who will be virtuously and peacefully contagious. Just as in the story of the woman caught in adultery, others in a vengeful crowd will then follow the first's example and also choose not to retaliate or participate in the logic of sacrifice, breaking the chain of retribution. Jesus's actions here and teaching elsewhere in the Gospels both reinforce these same points.

Conversion of insight, choosing good models, participation in a positively contagious community of love, and renunciation of retaliation and forgiveness of enemies will all lead to reducing violence if not eliminating it—both for ourselves individually and for us collectively as a human race. Today, with the sacrificial crisis running rampant around the globe, but where this violence of "things hidden since the foundation of the world" has been revealed, our choices are to participate in scapegoating and sacrifice or love and forgive instead. If we choose love and constructive models, what would the world look like?

To use examples we have discussed before earlier in the book, we might have a world where classmates would not envy each other over a pair of shoes, but might instead buy a poor classmate a pair of shoes; the two brothers, Lee and Austin, in *True West,* would not covet one another's possessions and personas but find reconciliation; the four lovers in *Midsummer Night's Dream*, rather than taking cruel vengeance upon one another, would console one another and live in friendship; the two tramps in *Waiting for Godot* would help Lucky and Pozzo rather than tormenting them; Cesar's cabinet might not gang up collectively as a mob and murder him but could find a peaceful political solution; and Lula would not murder Clay during the Civil Rights era but help forge new freedoms for others. In a reversal of the great sins depicted in the Bible, ultimately Cain would not envy and

---

21. Girard, *Things Hidden Since the Foundation of the World*, 199.

Conclusion

murder his brother Abel but help and learn from him; and Joseph's brothers would not envy and plot to kill him and sell him into slavery, but love him for his father's sake, enriching them all. This is the choice that awaits us: "We have to destroy one another or love one another, and humanity, we fear, will prefer to destroy itself. The future of the world is out of our control, and yet it is in our hands."[22]

We can participate in either constructive mimetic desire or destructive mimetic desire, but whichever we choose will overtake and transform us. Think about the many stories we have examined and see if they resonate with you; perhaps you can think of your own stories. All of us have them. Will you stay with the patterns of envy and rivalry that have so often been our human default position, leading to violence and scapegoating, or move toward peace offered by stories in the Gospels and in many insightful works of literature that show us the way, as Girard has shown. The choice is up to you. A better world awaits us.

---

22. Girard, *Battling to the End*, 48–49.

A Brief Glossary of Mimetic Theory

all-against-one—the process of a community gathering and ganging up against one person (or group of people) to accuse and cast the blame on them for their problem. See **scapegoat mechanism**.

contagion—in the mimetic process emerging from doubling, either constructive or harmful desire spreads itself to contaminate other individuals, other doubles, or society as a whole. Contagion can function simply, as in the fashion of the year, or it can function more on an abstract cultural level such as that found in ruthless envy, politics, or ideology. Examples would be the destructive contagion of people joining groups such as the KKK or World War II Nazism, or more positively, in those joining in peace movements against these groups. See **mimetic contagion**.

crisis of undifferentiation/sacrificial crisis—these are synonyms stressing different parts of the same process in which a community enters into a state of confusion where differences are lost (crisis of undifferentiation), which then leads to and results in a full-blown event in which a scapegoat is killed or expelled (sacrificial crisis).

culture—in Girard's thought, culture arises out of myth, prohibition, and ritual, which are phenomena born out of the scapegoat mechanism. Girard calls these "the pillars of culture," especially when talking about archaic societies.

deviated transcendency—Girard points out that we have the drive toward wanting being or transcendence, a connection with something larger than ourselves, but it can be directed toward the wrong mediators and objects. He sees this as a "deviation" or going astray from a good impulse toward a transcendent level. Deviated transcendency is another name for being stuck in destructive forms of mimetic desire. Examples would be anorexia, or following the violent characters in *A Clockwork Orange*.

doubles—when the subject and the model have undergone imitating each other to the extent that the subject and the model can no longer be differentiated, they appear as one and the same, like twins. Girard calls this "enemy doubles" or "doubles."

double mediation—the process whereby the subject and model rapidly imitate one another until the object of desire drops out and becomes of no importance. The focus of the subject begins instead to fall fully on fascination and rivalry with the model, and the two begin rivaling and imitating one another as doubles.

envy—desiring the object of desire the model or others have and not being able to obtain it.

external mediation—refers to the form of mediation taking place between the subject, model, and object where there is great social distance between the subject (s), model (m), and the object of desire (o). The larger the distance between the subject and model, the less likely will be the chances of friction or rivalry over the object of desire (o), because the model's objects (o) are unattainable by the subject.

founding murder—the establishment of a civilization upon the murder and sacrifice of an individual, twin, or double during a mimetic crisis of undifferentiation. See the murder of Abel by Cain or the myth of the foundation of Rome on the murder of Remus by his twin brother Romulus.

innermost mediation/intimate mediation—these are synonyms for a new concept of mediation Girard came up with in his last book, *Battling to the End*. Innermost mediation goes beyond external mediation because in this type of mediation the subject can draw *close* to the mediator without rivalry. This closeness is possible because what the mediator wants is the well-being of the subject. This is a way of talking about love. Girard's example for this is the loving desire for us by God; or of Jesus's example in imitating God in a loving relation without grasping; or of saints and others who love like Jesus, who we can imitate.

internal mediation—refers to the form of mediation taking place between the subject (s), model (m), and object (o) where the social distance between the subject and the model is small and thus easily vulnerable to rivalry over possession of the object of desire (o). The smaller the distance between the

A Brief Glossary of Mimetic Theory

subject and the model in the mimetic triangle, the greater the possibility of friction and rivalry, because they can vie and compete for the same objects of desire.

kingdom of God—this is a term used in the Gospels to announce Jesus's new way of being, one which we are invited to join. Another name for a positively contagious community.

mimetic contagion—see **contagion**.

mimetic desire—a desire that is a result of imitation of another person's desire; an imitative desire; from the Greek word "mimesis" meaning imitation. The trajectory of a desire is a triangle, where the subject (s) looks at the model (m) to see what the model desires, the object of desire (o), in order to desire it.

mimetic theory—a name for the entirety of René Girard's life's work in which he discovers, develops, and explores the implications of mimetic desire, beginning with his first book *Deceit, Desire, and the Novel*. Girard's other books can be found in the footnotes and bibliography.

mimetic triangle—a synonym for **triangular desire.**

mediator—synonym for model. The one who suggests the object of desire (o) and thus causes the subject (s) to desire it.

model—a person or group of people who stand out in the subject's view and perspective as the guide towards a concrete or more abstract, metaphysical object. See **triangular desire**.

mimetic doubling—the process where the subject and the model imitate and rival each other for the object at hand, so rapidly and continuously that it cannot be stopped, turning each person into identical images or **doubles** of the other.

model-obstacle—a situation in which the subject attempts to imitate the model but this becomes very difficult or impossible to do because the model blocks the way the more the subject tries to imitate them.

myth—in Girard's thought, the story of the sacrificial crisis told from the perspective of the persecutors. The community comes to believe that the victim was responsible for the crisis. Myth is this strong belief in the victim's guilt and power to generate a crisis; the story the community tells itself about these events that mystifies them.

A Brief Glossary of Mimetic Theory

novelistic conversion—an individual's recognition and coming to terms with negative and destructive forms of mimetic desire and then changing it for good and constructive forms of mimetic desire. This term was part of Girard's first book *Deceit, Desire and the Novel*, where he saw how the heroes of the novels may recognize their pattern of destructive mimetic desire and undergo a metamorphosis. Girard says the novelist too undergoes this "conversion" or shift in point of view, a process which enables them to write the novel accurately representing destructive mimetic desire.

object of desire (object)—a physical thing or more abstract goal that a model has or desires that a subject then also desires. See **mimetic desire** and **triangular desire**.

prohibition—the taboo against imitating any aspect of the sacrificial crisis or scapegoat's characteristics. Prohibition is designed to keep the crisis of undifferentiation from happening again.

Passion—the death and resurrection of Jesus Christ.

ritual— selectively and deliberately imitating aspects of the sacrificial crisis or scapegoat's characteristics. The community believes the scapegoat had the power to create the peace the community feels after the scapegoat is killed or expelled, and so tries to harness the victim's power by imitating certain actions repeatedly.

rivalry— the active state of conflict or competition between a subject (s) and model (m) over possession of the exact same object (o) that cannot be shared between them.

romantic lie—the name Girard gives to the belief or illusion that we are independent, autonomous subjects, not subjects who imitate others or a model; a false reality that we create and live in. He points out that this is a common feature of modern life. This term comes from his first book, *Deceit, Desire and the Novel*.

scapegoat—an individual or group of people who are accused and blamed for the mimetic crisis or plague that has affected and spread within the community.

scapegoat mechanism—the process and mechanism whereby everyone in the community gathers and gangs up against an innocent victim or group, accusing them for the problem. The innocent victim is then either sacrificed (killed) or expelled to solve the crisis. Girard argues that Jesus's death and resurrection unveiled the workings of the scapegoat mechanism, so it no longer works as well as it did in archaic times. Also known as the victimage mechanism.

subject—the person in the mimetic triangle who imitates the model—what the model does, has, or desires. See **triangular desire.**

surrogate victim—a synonym for **scapegoat.**

Satan —"Satan" in the Bible literally means "accuser." It also can mean "tempter" or "seducer," as seen in the story of Adam and Eve in the book of Genesis. In Girard's reading of the Bible, Satan refers not to a specific personal diabolical supernatural being but (based on the witness of the text itself) specifically refers to the processes of order and disorder in the sacrificial crisis within the community, along with the sacrifice of an accused scapegoat. As Girard stresses, "Satan" has no "being" like humans; it is a process, so it cannot be referred to with the pronouns "he" or "she," but only "it." Satan is another name for the **scapegoat mechanism** itself.

triangular desire—the structure of mimetic desire with a subject (s) viewing and imitating the model's (m) desires for an object of desire (o). In the mimetic triangle the model mediates the subject's desires as the subject follows and desires that which the model has and/or desires. Also known as **mimetic triangle.**

vertical transcendency—in our quest for more being or to be in touch with something greater than ourselves, we can become oriented more authentically toward God or a way of love, positive contagion, and forgiveness. This involves looking away from those models nearest us who tempt us to envy them.

A Biographical Introduction to René Girard

CONSIDERED ONE OF THE foremost thinkers of our time in the fields of anthropology, religion, literature and psychology, René Girard was born on Christmas day in Avignon, France, in 1923. He obtained his Baccalaureate in Philosophy from Lycée of Avignon in 1941 and attended the École des Chartres in Paris from 1943 to 1947, graduating as an *archeiviste-paléographe*, a specialist in medieval studies.

Following his 1947 graduation, Girard came to the United States, where he enrolled at Indiana University in the Department of History and obtained his second PhD in 1950. Shifting from medieval studies to contemporary history, his second PhD thesis focused on the twentieth century: "American Opinion of France, 1940–1943." Following his degree, he taught at Indiana University, Duke University, Bryn Mawr College and Johns Hopkins University.

In 1959, while working on his first book, *Mensonge romantique et vérité Romanesque* (published in 1961 and in translation, *Deceit, Desire and the Novel: Self and Other in Literary Structure* in 1965), Girard underwent a conversion to Christianity. While touched upon in his first book, *Deceit, Desire and the Novel*, Girard did not fully delve into the Christian faith until his third book, *Des choses caches depuis la foundation du monde* (published in 1978 and in translation, *Things Hidden Since the Foundation of the World* in 1987). This book's three parts focus on i) anthropology, ii) the Judaeo-Christian Scriptures, and iii) interdividual psychology. Girard's non-sacrificial reading of the Scriptures in *Things Hidden Since the Foundation of the World* created a massive scandal in the academic circles in both Europe as well as the United States.

A Biographical Introduction to René Girard

In addition to his distinguished positions and role as Chair of Johns Hopkins' Department of Romance Languages (1965 to 1968), Girard was also one of the literary critics who introduced the field of structuralist literary criticism to the United States. While serving as Chair in 1966, along with Richard Macksey and Eugenio Donato, Girard organized a conference entitled "The Structuralist Controversy: The Languages of Criticism and the Sciences of Man." The conference included such figures as Jacques Derrida, Jacque Lacan, Roland Barthes, Lucien Goldman, Jean Hyppolite and Tsvetan Todorov, among others.

In 1971 Girard accepted a distinguished professor position at the State University of New York at Buffalo, where he taught until 1976, when he returned to Johns Hopkins as the John M. Beall Professor of the Humanities. While at Johns Hopkins, *La violence et le sacré* was published (in 1972 and in translation, as *Violence and the Sacred*, in 1977). This book, which focused on the anthropological fundamentals of the mimetic theory and mythological structures, brought critical attention from anthropologists, psychologists and literary critics. In 1981 Girard began teaching as the Andrew Hammond Professor of French Languages, Literature and Civilization at Stanford University's Department of French Literature and Languages, as well as in the school's Department of Comparative Literature. In 1990 the Colloquium on Violence and Religion (COV&R) was formed by a group of twenty-five researchers and scholars of mimetic theory, and continues to meet annually throughout Europe, the world and the United States.[1]

Girard received countless prizes and degrees during his lifetime, including honorary doctorates from Vrije University, Amsterdam (1985), University of Innsbruck, Austria (1988), University d'Anvers, Belgium (1995), University of Padova, Italy (2001), University of Montréal, Canada (2004) and University of St. Andrews, United Kingdom (2008). A partial list of Girard's many awards includes the Guggenheim in both 1960 and 1967, the Modern Language Association (MLA) Award in 1965, the Prix Médicis essaie for *Shakespeare, les feux de l'envie* in 1990, Grand Prix de philosophie de l'Acadamie Française pour ensemble de son oeuvre in 1996, Nonjno literary prize in Italy in 1998, Prix Aujourd'hui for *Les origins de la culture* in 2004 and the Dr. Leopold-Lucas-Preis in 2006. In addition, in 1998 Girard was awarded the Modern Language Association MLA Lifetime award and inducted to the Académie Française. More than ever, in

---

1. The COVER web page describing events and annual colloquium meetings can be found at http://www.uibk.ac.at/theol/cover/.

recent years the mimetic theory has held great attention, and a prestigious and well-recognized position amongst academics as well as enthusiasts of popular culture, popular psychology, comparative religion and, last but not least, spirituality. René Girard retired from Stanford University in 1995 and continued to live at Stanford with his wife, Martha where he continued to write until he passed away in 2015.

Bibliography

Ackerman, Andy, dir. *Seinfeld*. Season 9, episode 17, "The Bookstore." Aired April 9, 1998, on NBC.
Artistotle. *Poetics*. Translated by S. H. Butcher. Introduction by Francis Fergusson. New York: Hill and Wang, 1961.
Bailie, Gil. *Violence Unveiled: Humanity at the Crossroads*. New York: Crossroad, 1995.
Bandera, Cesáreo. *The Sacred Game: The Role of the Sacred in the Genesis of Modern Fiction*. University Park: Pennsylvania State University Press, 1994.
Bateson, Gregory, et al. *Steps to an Ecology of the Mind*. New York: Ballantine, 1972.
Beckett, Samuel. *I Can't Go On. I'll Go On*. New York: Grove, 1976.
———. *Waiting For Godot*. New York: Grove, 1954.
Burgis, Luke. *Wanting: The Power of Mimetic Desire In Everyday Life*. New York: St. Martin's Press, 2021.
Burkert, Walter, et al. *Violent Origins: Walter Burkert, René Girard and Jonathan Z. Smith on Ritual Killing and Cultural Formation*. Edited by Robert G. Hamerton-Kelly. Stanford, CA: Stanford University Press, 1987.
Canetti, Elias. *Crowds and Power*. Translated by Carol Stewart. Repr. New York: Farrar, Straus, and Giroux, 1973.
Carel, Havi, and David Gamez. *What Philosophy Is*. London and New York: Continuum, 2004.
Carleson, Marvin. *Theories of the Theatre: A Historical and Critical Survey from the Greeks to the Present*. Ithaca, NY: Cornell University Press, 1984.
Cervantes, Miguel de. *Don Quixote*. Translated by J. M. Cohen. New York: Penguin, 1950.
Chantre, Benoît. "The Steeple of Combray: From 'Vertical' To 'Deviated' Transcendence." Translated by Trevor Cribbon Merrill. *Religion and Literature* 43 (2011) 158–164.
Cobb, Humphrey. *Paths of Glory*. Introduction by James H. Meredith. New York: Penguin, 2010.
Davies, Nigel. *Human Sacrifice*. New York: William Morrow and Company, 1981.
Depoortere, Frederick. *Christ in Modern Philosophy: Gianni Vattimo, René Girard and Slavoj Zizěk*. London: New York: T. & T. Clark, 2008.
Derrida, Jacques. *Dissemination*. Translated by Barbara Johnson. Chicago: University of Chicago Press, 1981.
———. *Margins of Philosophy*. Translated by Alan Bass. Chicago: University of Chicago Press, 1982.

Bibliography

———. *Writing and Difference*. Translated by Alan Bass. Chicago: University of Chicago Press, 1978.

Donato, Eugenio, and Richard Macksey, eds. *The Structuralist Controversy: The Languages of Criticism and the Sciences of Man*. Baltimore: Johns Hopkins University Press, 1970.

Dumouchel, Paul. *Violence and Truth: On the Work of René Girard*. London: The Athlone, 1988.

Dupuy, Jean-Pierre. *Ordres et désordres. Enquéte sur un nouveau paradigme*. Paris: Ed. du Seuil, 1982.

———. *La marque du sacré*. Paris: Carnets nord, 2008.

———. *La panique*. 1e éd. Paris: François-Xavier de Guibert, 2010.

———. *Self-deception and paradoxes of rationality*. Edited by Jean-Pierre Dupuy. Stanford, CA: CSLI Publications, 1998.

Euripedes. *Euripedes V*. Edited by David Grene and Richmond Lattimore. Chicago: The University of Chicago Press, 1959.

Flatley, Louise. "Why 'A Clockwork Orange' Was Banned . . . by Stanley Kubrick Himself." *The Vintage News*, February 5, 2019. https://www.thevintagenews.com/2019/02/05/a-clockwork-orange/.

Fleming, Chris. *René Girard, Violence and Mimesis*. Cambridge: Polity, 2004.

Freccero, John. *Dante: Poetics of Conversion*. Cambridge, MA: Harvard University Press, 1986.

Freud, Sigmund. *Civilization and Its Discontents*. Translated by James Strachey. New York: W.W. Norton, 1961.

———. *The Interpretation of Dreams*. Translated by Joyce Clark. New York: Oxford University Press. 1999.

———. *On Dreams*. Translated by James Strachey. New York: W.W. Norton, 1980.

Girard, René. *Achever Clausewitz*. Paris: Carnets nord, 2007.

———. *Anorexie et désir mimétique*. Éditions de L'Herne, 2008.

———. *Anorexia and Mimetic Desire*. Translated by Mark R. Anspach. Edited by William A. Johnsen. East Lansing: Michigan State University Press, 2013.

———. *Battling to the End: Conversations with Benoît Chantre*. East Lansing: Michigan State University Press, 2010.

———. *Le bouc émissaire*. Paris: Grasset, 1982.

———. *Celui par qui le scandale arrive: entretiens avec Maria Stella Barberi*. Paris: Descalée de Brouwer, 2001.

———. *René Girard et le problème du mal*. Edited by Michel Deguy and Jean-Pierre Dupuy. Paris: B. Grasset, 1982.

———. *Des choses cachées depuis la fondation du monde*. Paris: Grasset, 1978.

———. *Critique dans un souterrain*. Lausanne: L'Age d'Homme, 1976.

———. *La contraddizione virtuosa: il problema educativo, Don Milani e Il Forteto / a cura di Giuseppe Fornari, Nicola Casanova; con un'intervista a René Girard*. Bologna: Il mulino, 2008.

———. *Le départ de Jeanne Darc: drame historique en deux actes et en vers: précédé de sa biographie d'après des documents authentiques et du plan de ses ennemis jusqu'à nos jours: dédiés à la jeunesse française*. = Paris: Librairie Centrale des Publications Populaires, 1879.

———. *Deceit, Desire, and the Novel: Self and Other in Literary Structure*. Translated by Yvonne Freccero. Baltimore: The Johns Hopkins University Press, 1965.

Bibliography

———. *Dieu, une invention?* Éditions de l'Atelier. With André Gounelle and Alain Houziaux, 2007.

———. *Dostoïevski, du double à l'unité.* Paris: Plon, 1963.

———. *Evolution and Conversion: Dialogues on the Origins of Culture.* René Girard with Pierpaolo Antonello and João Cezar de Castro Rocha. New York: T. & T. Clark, 2007.

———. *The Girard Reader.* Edited by James G. Williams. New York: Crossroad, 1996.

———. *I See Satan Fall Like Lightning.* Translated by James Williams. Maryknoll, NY: Orbis, 2001.

———. *Je vois Satan tomber comme l'éclair.* Paris: Grasset, 1999.

———. *Job: The Victim of His People.* Translated by Yvonne Freccero. Stanford, CA: Stanford University Press, 1987.

———. *Lenz, 1751–1792, genèse d'une dramaturgie du tragi-comique.* Paris: C. Klincksieck, 1968.

———. *Mensonge romantique et vérité romanesque.* Paris: Grasset, 1961.

———. *Mimesis and Theory: Essays on Literature and Criticism, 1953–2005.* Edited with an introduction by Robert Doran. Stanford, CA: Stanford University Press, 2008.

———. *Oedipus Unbound: Selected Writings on Rivalry and Desire.* Edited by Mark Anspach. Stanford, CA: Stanford University Press, 2004.

———. *Les origines de la culture. Entretiens avec Pierpaolo Antonello et João Cezar de Castro Rocha.* Paris: Desclée de Brouwer, 2004.

———. *Proust: A Collection of Critical Essays.* Englewood Cliffs: Prentice Hall, 1962.

———. *Proust: A Collection of Critical Essays.* Edited by René Girard. Westport, CT: Greenwood, 1977.

———. *Quand ces choses commenceront.* Paris: Arléa, 1994.

———. *Rencontres internationales de Genève (37th: 1999).* Lausanne: L'Age d'homme, 2000.

———. *Resurrection from the Underground: Feodor Dostoevsky.* Translated by James G. Williams. New York: Crossroad, 1997.

———. *La route antique des hommes pervers.* Paris: Grasset, 1985.

———. *Le sacrifice.* Paris: Bibliothèque nationale de France, 2003.

———. *Sacrifice.* Translated by Matthew Pattillo and David Dawson. Edited by William A. Johnsen. East Lansing: Michigan State University Press, 2011.

———. *The Scapegoat.* Translated by Yvonne Freccero. Baltimore: The Johns Hopkins University Press, 1986.

———. *Shakespeare: A Theatre of Envy.* Repr. St. Augustine's Press, 2004.

———. *To Double Business Bound: Essays on Literature, Mimesis, and Anthropology.* Baltimore: Johns Hopkins University Press, 1978.

———. *To Honor René Girard, Presented on the Occasion of His Sixtieth Birthday by Colleagues, Students, Friends.* Saratoga, CA: Anba Libri 1986.

———. *Le tragique et la pitié: discours de réception de René Girard à l'Académie française et réponse de Michel Serres.* Paris: Pommier, 2007.

———. *Verità o fede debole. Dialogo su cristianesimo e relativismo.* Transeuropa Edizioni, Massa. 2006.

———. *Violence and the Sacred.* Translated by Patrick Gregory. Baltimore: The Johns Hopkins University Press, 1977.

———. *Violence and the Sacred, and Things Hidden. A Discussion with René Girard at Esprit (1973).* Translated by Andrew J. McKenna. East Lansing: Michigan State University Press, 2022.

Bibliography

———. *De la violence à la divinité*. Contains *mensonge romantique et vérité romanesque, La violence et le sacré, Des choses cachées depuis la fondation du monde* and *Le bouc émissaire*, with a new general introduction. Paris: Grasset. 2007

———. *La violence et le sacré*. Paris: Grasset, 1972.

———. *La voix méconnue du reel; Une théorie des mythes archaïqueus et modernes*. Traduit de l'anglais par Bee Formentelli. Paris: Editions Bernard Grasset & Fasquelle, 2002.

Girard, René, et al. *Architects and Mimetic Rivalry*. Edited by Younés, Samir. Great Britain: Papadakis, 2012.

Girard, René, with Jean-Michel Oughourlian and Guy Lefort *Things Hidden Since the Foundation of the World*. Translated by Stephen Bann (Books II & III) and Michael Metteer (Book I). London: Athelon, 1987.

Goodhart, Sandor. *Sacrificing Commentary: Reading the End of Literature*. Baltimore and London: The Johns Hopkins University Press, 1996.

Golding, William. *The Lord of the Flies*. New York: Penguin, 1954.

Grene, David, and Richmond Lattimore, ed. *The Complete Greek Tragedies: Aeschylus I: Oresteia*, Translated by Richmond Lattimore. Chicago and London: The University of Chicago Press, 1953.

———. *The Complete Greek Tragedies: Sophocles I: Oedipus the King*. Translated by David Grene, *Oedipus at Colonus*, Translated by Robert Fitzegerald, *Antigone*, Translated by Elizabeth Wyckoff. Chicago and London: The University of Chicago Press, 1954.

Grivois, Henri, and Jean-Pierre Dupuy. *Mécanismes mentaux, mécanismes sociaux: de la psychose à la panique*. Paris: La Découverte, 1995.

Gumbrecht, Hans Ulrich. *Making Sense in Life and Literature*. Translated by Glen Burns. Minneapolis: University of Minnesota Press, 1992.

Hatch, James V., and Ted Shine, eds. *Black Theatre USA, Plays By African American: The Recent Period, 1935-Today*. New York: The Free Press, 1974.

Herrin, Marcia, and Nancy Matsumoto. *A Parent's Guide to Eating Disorders*. Carlsbad, CA: Gruze, 2007.

Jackson, Shirley. *Novels and Stories: The Lottery, The Haunting of Hill House, We Have Always Lived in the Castle, Other Stories and Sketches*. New York: Penguin Putnam, 2010.

Jones, Ernest. *The Life and Work of Sigmund Freud*. Edited and abridged by Lionel Trilling and Steven Marcus. New York: Basic, 1961.

Kierkegarrd, Søren. *Fear and Trembling*. Edited by C. Stephen Evans and Sylvia Walsh. Translated by Sylvia Walsh. Cambridge: Cambridge University Press, 2006.

———. *Sickness Unto Death*. Translated by Howard V. Hong and Edna H. Hong. Princeton: Princeton University Press, 1980.

Kirwan, Michael. *Discovering Girard*. Cambridge, MA: Cowley, 2005.

———. *Girard and Theology*. New York: T. & T. Clark, 2009.

Kott, Jan. *Shakespeare Our Contemporary*. Translated by Boleslaw Taborski. New York: W.W. Norton, 1974.

Kubrick, Stanley, dir. *Paths of Glory*. Culver City, CA: United Artists, 1989.

Kubrick, Stanley, and Jim Thompson. *Paths of Glory*. https://www.screenwritersnetwork.org/wp-content/uploads/2021/03/Paths-Of-Glory-Script.pdf

Kurosawa, Akira. *Seven Samurai and Other Screenplays*. Translation of *Ikiru* in the collection by Donald Richi. London: Faber and Faber, 1992.

Livingston, Paisley. *Ingmar Bergman and the Ritual of Art*. Ithaca and London: Cornell University Press, 1982.

Bibliography

McKenna, Andrew J. *Violence and Difference: Girard, Derrida, and Deconstruction*. Chicago: University of Illinois Press, 1992.

Mulder, Jack, Jr. *Kierkegaard and the Catholic Tradition: Conflict and Dialogue*. Bloomington: Indiana University Press, 2010

Nastuk, Matthew. *The Simpsons*. Season 22, episode 14, "Angry Dad: The Movie." Aired February 20, 2011 on FOX.

Nietzsche, Friedrich. *The Birth of Tragedy* and *The Case of Wagner*. Translated and commentary by Walter Kaufmann. New York: Vintage, 1967.

———. *On the Genealogy of Morals* and *Ecco Homo*. Translated by and edited by Walter Kaufmann. New York: Vintage, 1967.

———. *The Will to Power: A New Translation*. Translated by Walter Kaufmann and R. J. Hollingdale. Edited by Walter Kaufmann. London: Weidenfeld & Nicolson, 1968.

Nuest, Kevin. "Michael Jordan." *My Hero*, June 9, 2004. http://www.myhero.com/myhero/hero.asp?hero=m_jordan.

O'Neill, Eugene. *Complete Plays 1913–1920*. New York: Literary Classics of the United States, 1988.

Osborn, Carly. *The Theory of René Girard, A Very Simple Introduction*. Melbourne: Australian Girard Seminar: 2016.

Oughourlian, Jean-Michel. *Genèse du désir*. Paris: Carnets nord, 2007.

———. *The Genesis of Desire*. Translated by Eugene Webb. East Lansing: Michigan State University Press, 2010.

———. *The Mimetic Brain*. Translated by Trevor Cribben Merrill. East Lansing: Michigan State University Press, 2016.

———. *Un mime nommé désir: hystérie, transe, possession, adorcisme*. Paris: B. Grasset, 1982.

———. *The Puppet of Desire: The Psychology of Hysteria, Possession, and Hypnosis*. Translated by Eugene Webb. Stanford, CA: Stanford University Press, 1991.

Robinson, Peter. "Interview with René Girard, 'Uncommon Knowledge.'" Hoover Tower, Stanford University, December 10, 2009. http://www.nationalreview.com/corner/191248/girard-and-modern-world/peter-robinson.

Serres, Michel. *Detachment*. Translated from the French by Genevieve James and Raymond Federman. Athens: Ohio University Press, 1989.

———. *Genesis*. Translated by Geneviève James and James Nielson. Ann Arbor: University of Michigan Press, 1995.

———. *La guerre mondiale*. Paris: Le Pommier, 2008.

———. *Hermes: Literature, Science, Philosophy*. Edited by Josué V. Harari and David F. Bell. Baltimore: Johns Hopkins University Press, 1982.

———. *Parasite*. Translated by Lawrence R. Schehr. Minneapolis: University of Minnesota Press, 2007.

———. *Rome: The Book of Foundations*. Translated by Felicia McCarren. Stanford, CA: Stanford University Press, 1991.

———. *Temps des crises*. Paris: Le Pommier, 2009.

Shaffer, Peter. *Amadeus*. New York: Harper and Row, 1981.

Shakespeare, William. *The Riverside Shakespeare*. Edited by G. Blakemore Evans and J. J. M. Tobin. 2nd ed. Boston: Houghton Mifflin, 1997.

Shepard, Sam. *Seven Plays*. New York: Bantam, 1981.

Sophocles. *Oedipus the King*. Edited by David Grene and Richmond Lattimore. Chicago: University of Chicago Press, 1991.

Bibliography

Telander, Rick. "Senseless." *Vault*, May 14, 1990. https://vault.si.com/vault/1990/05/14/senseless-in-americas-cities-kids-are-killing-kids-over-sneakers-and-other-sports-apparel-favored-by-drug-dealers-whos-to-blame.

Twain, Mark. *Tom Sawyer*. Maidenhead, 1975.

Weil, Simone. *Gravity and Grace*. Translated by Emma Craufurd and Mario von der Ruher. London and New York: Routlege, 1952.

Wenders, Wim, and Handke, Peter. *Der Himmel Uber Berlin, Ein Filmbuch*. Berlin: Suhrkamp Verlag, 1987.

Wood, D. R., et al., eds. *The Bible Dictionary (Third Edition)*. Leicester: Universities and Colleges Christian Fellowship, 1996.

www.ingramcontent.com/pod-product-compliance
Lightning Source LLC
Chambersburg PA
CBHW071821230426
43670CB00013B/2523